GARETH

Long kicks from scrum-halves are the quickest and most decisive way to turn defence into attack. That proved the case on my last visit to Twickenham in 1978. The ground was muddy and the rain had greased the ball. How could we get up to the English end of the field to break the 6–all deadlock? I managed to kick from our 25 to theirs, a long screw that torpedoed into the turf and sprung sideways into touch. We kept them there and ten minutes later Phil Bennett was kicking the penalty from thirty yards to win.

One or two of the English boys that night grabbed me by the throat, playfully of course, and said, 'You little Welsh b——, your kick was the one that killed us.'

GARETH

Gareth Edwards

ARROW BOOKS

Arrow Books Ltd
3 Fitzroy Square, London w1p 6jd

An imprint of the Hutchinson Publishing Group

London Melbourne Sydney Auckland
Wellington Johannesburg and agencies
throughout the world

First published by Stanley Paul 1978
Arrow edition 1979

Made and printed in Great Britain
by The Anchor Press Ltd
Tiptree, Essex

isbn 0 09 921190 4

Contents

To Maureen, my parents, Jack Hamer and the many
people who have been behind me all the way.

Acknowledgements

I should like to thank Tony Lewis for his invaluable
help with the writing of this book.

Thanks are also due to the following for allowing the
use of copyright photographs: The Cape Argus, Color-
sport, Derek Evans, Presse Sports, John Rubython,
South Wales Evening Post, Sunday Express Johannesburg, Wellington Evening Post, Western Mail & Echo.

GE

I

Beginning at the end

The bus carrying the Welsh team and officials was quickly escorted through the crawling lines of traffic around Twickenham. Welsh supporters waved and cheered. The rain did not touch their spirits. Now those are the dedicated ones, I thought.

Take a man like Hywel Awful, my old pal from Gwaun-cae-Gurwen. He had turned up in London the night before, quite by surprise. I had not seen him for years because he had left the village and moved a long way west, down to Pembrokeshire. 'I've brought you a couple of tickets for the game Gareth,' he offered. 'Being as it's special for you, y'know, your fiftieth. Thought you'd need some.'

I certainly did. 'You've got enough for yourself Awful haven't you?' I asked.

Big Hywel, best mixer of fishing paste west of Swansea, said, 'No, I don't think I'll go, Gar. I'm going to watch it on tele in the hotel. Twickenham is such a long way out, isn't it.'

I laughed at that again on the bus. It was one helluva trip from Pembrokeshire. You would think he would make the last lap to the ground. Lots of others had. When they saw us the ranks of red and white on the pavements all responded, even sang, then lowered their heads back into the rain, set on their pilgrimage to watch Wales beat England, my countrymen's eternal dream.

Hywel Awful had been right; this was a special day

for me. I had played every game for Wales since my
first cap in Paris back in 1967. Today was the fiftieth.
No Welshman had got that far.

The bus splashed through the West Stand car park.
They were all there – the Englishmen, lunching from
the boots of their cars, trimmed moustaches, British
Warm overcoats, sensible shoes, chicken legs, red or
white wine and a tot of 'nonsense' for the match. Gerald
Davies, who had been with me from the start, looked
his usual tense self, whiter than white. My stomach was
in knots too. Fear of failure had set in. Losing at Twickenham is more than coming second in a rugby match. It
is a national disaster.

'Why do we keep on doing this Gareth?' Gerald
asked, not really expecting an answer.

I muttered something like, 'I don't know, but all I do
know is that we'll be out there with them one day soon,
tucking into the home-made pie and champers.'

I took in the whole scene as the bus slowed and the
Welsh boys reached for their kit. The lads had been
superb. A lot of attention had been focused on me in the
press and television during the week of build-up, and
telegrams had poured into the hotel, yet they understood. I was afraid it might disturb them, but they were
too experienced for that. They took all the fuss in their
stride and I was glad about it.

Rain rushed down the window of the bus. There was
a young lad holding his father's hand, all smiles in his
red and white bobble hat. I had never been taken to
Twickenham to see Wales play at that age, but I used
to stand and stare at the Cwmgors team at home won-
dering if I would ever be big enough to play for them.
Suddenly everything went through my mind before that
fiftieth cap – the Swansea valley, Gwaun-cae-Gurwen,
Colbren Square where everybody knew everybody. . . .

2

Gwaun-cae-Gurwen

I look around and laugh quite loudly to think how I must have been; a short, dark little fellow, buzzing around in everyone's way. I can't remember walking too often. People, shops, paving stones flashed past me. I think I ran everywhere, even when I was very young and living in Ger-yr-Afon, the road near the river.

I was only five years old then, but I would race after the big Cwmgors boys as they went up to the field to play rugby, and make them carry me over the stream on their backs so that I could watch them. I loved it when they kicked the ball high; so high it seemed to disappear. 'Duw! Kick it over the clouds boys,' I used to shout. I really thought it went over the clouds. What a menace I must have been; and rugby football a handling game too!

We were not particularly a rugby family, though everyone in Gwaun-cae-Gurwen, or any other village in the South Wales valleys for that matter, knew something about the game. If a local boy had been invited down the valley to turn out for the Scarlets, the All Whites or the Blacks (Llanelli, Swansea or Neath) he would return with new stature. I distinctly remember seeing Arwyn Morris, a Cwmgors forward who had the traditional afflictions of a valley prop – wide shoulders, a short neck and a cauliflower ear, walking down the street one day. Off I went again, like a whippet. I ran flat out so that this rugby giant might say to himself, 'Darro! That lad's fast.' I suppose I always acted as if I

9

wanted them to say about me, as they said about Arwyn Morris, that they were proud to know me.

My father never really had a chance to play a lot of rugby. He had to go underground at the age of fourteen, spent the early part of his life as a miner and later changed to the buses. The war interrupted his life like it did many others, but my mother always felt that at the back of his couldn't-care-less attitude to the game was the death of his father. My grandfather, Jacob Edwards, played a lot of rugby. After one match he caught a heavy cold. In those days there were no shower baths. You just played, towelled down and then cooled off at the pub over a few pints. His cold turned to pneumonia and, very soon after that match, Jacob Edwards was dead.

Mind you, my Dad has always done everything to encourage my rugby, but he had only been to a Welsh match once before I played. That was in Cardiff, and even then I think he only went because he was driving a bus-load of people there.

However, every Christmas I got my new jersey and socks and perhaps boots and ball as well. I always asked for the Welsh colours, but my mother used to come back saying that she could not get red. Once she got red and white stripes and at least they were the Cwmgors colours, cherry and white. Once I remember having Newport colours (I can just hear that great old Cardiff prop forward, Stan Bowes, saying, if he reads this, 'Now fancy, he had been one of these Newport black-and-amber bastards all the time'). But the miracle happened one Christmas morning: there they were, an all-red jersey and white shorts. I ran straight up the field, the farmer's field.

The farmer's name was Archie, and Archie's field was just a narrow strip, about twenty yards wide, all reeds on one side and a railway bank on the other which we called the East Terrace. We had unbelievable games there. Somehow all the boys in the village fitted into it. We put coats down for goal posts. Then when

Archie the farmer chased us off it, about once every fortnight, we had to scramble away. But he must have seen the carefully laid sawdust touchlines and try-lines. Very professional. *Cae* is the Welsh word for field, and *Cae Archie* is therefore Archie's field. It is funny nowadays, say in Cardiff, to talk to an old pal from G-c-G and refer to *Cae Archie*, because people who do not speak Welsh think we are claiming to have nipped over to Pakistan for a game of rugby!

So that Christmas, dressed in my Welsh jersey, I got my younger brother Gethin out of the house to play on *Cae Archie*. Gethin had rugby talent. One of the richest experiences in my whole career was partnering him at half-back in the Cardiff first team during the 1972 season, especially against Rhodesia on our tour. But Gethin is, and always was, reluctant. As boys, if it was in any way cold – and you needed to be hardy up towards the top of the Swansea Valley – Geth would only come out if he could put on his balaclava, trousers and pullover. At the first drop of rain he would be back inside warming himself in front of the fire for an hour. That Christmas Day I was ready to take on the world, yet there was no one to play with. Most of the lads were not allowed out to play on Christmas Day, and the only ones I saw were having a spin on their new bikes. So I walked home, cheesed off. My kit was clean. No one had tackled me. My jersey smelled of the shop and the creases in the sleeves were sharp enough to cut a wing forward in half. My knees were not even dirty. Then I looked up the road and down. There was no one around. I crouched down low, eyeing and sniffing the huge pool on the mud pathway like a sheepdog stalking. Next moment I was in it, a diving try; baptizing my new kit, but making sure that my hands stretched out far enough to get the safe touch-down ... after all, it was the last minute of the match ... England 5 Wales 6. I felt better after that!

We moved house when I was about six years old to another part of the village called Colbren Square. Life continued as always with plenty of play, and only a moaning acceptance of school, the Gwaun-cae-Gurwen Primary School until I was eleven and then the Secondary Modern to the age of thirteen.

To me Colbren Square was a fifty-five-yard pitch of concrete road and pavement. The grandstands were the small houses and gardens on each side. One end was sealed by a T-junction and there was no traffic there in those days. More international rugby matches, more soccer cup finals, more test cricket matches were played there than on any of the world's great grounds. Every hedge was a high hurdle to be taken at speed; every driveway was a long-jump pit and the crack in the pavement before the gap was the take-off board. I just had to hit it in full stride. Often, if I was on my own, I would leap in the air and head an imaginary goal through someone's front window.

There were lots of boys in the neighbourhood but one of my sportsmad pals lived opposite. Huw Davies, now called Huw Eic after his father Eic Davis who is well known as a Welsh language sports broadcaster for BBC Wales. Huw is a Welsh language newsreader with HTV – a bit of opposition in the family.

If I had a rugby ball or a soccer ball for Christmas, it was worn out by February, bald and split down the seams. It was the same old story . . . 'Two minutes to go . . . England are leading . . . it's a penalty to Wales,' says the self-appointed commentator . . . 'And it's Huw Davies placing the ball just inside the English half. Can he make it? It's been a wonderful day here at Cardiff Arms Park with England leading Wales by 13 point to 12. This must be the last kick of the match.'

Huw would slowly pick his clods of earth from between the paving stones and make his nest on the roadway on which to tee up the ball. 'Inside the English half,' means that it was only twenty yards from the posts. In fact, there was only one post, the lamp-post.

If you took an imaginary line across from the top of that lamp-post to an imaginary lamp-post on the other side of the road then you had visions of the uprights and the crossbar. The uprights *above* the bar only came into the mind if England were kicking for goal and there had to be some proper geometrical reason for disallowing it. Inevitably English kicks rebounded off posts into Welsh arms.

I can see Huw now, measuring back his step; drawing in deep breaths and looking up at the goal. I realize now too that Mrs Davies in the end house was holding her breath as well, waiting for the ball to land in her garden again. It only had to touch her front door and – whoop – the door was open and the ball gone.

Wales were invincible for many years with an imperishable ground record on Colbren Square. The only reverses suffered were from neighbours like Mrs Davies. One day I took a real swipe at the ball, but I was Manchester United this time so it had to be a great shot. However my shoe flew off and went straight through her window. We got up the courage to knock on the door and ask for my shoe back, and Mrs Davies reckoned that it landed right in the middle of a cake she was baking. We offered to pay for the breakage, and so we did out of our own pocket money. My father saw to that. 'You repair it too,' he thundered. We got glass from Brynamman and put it in ourselves.

My father had the sort of authority you would never dare oppose. His voice was a low and *basso profundo* 'Come here,' or 'Go there.' When we were playing late down the field and it was getting dark, he would let loose one of his famous whistles across the rooftops from streets away. 'Gareth. 'Ome.'

'Winning goal, Dad,' I would yell back.

'Right,' he would always come back with great understanding. 'Five minutes.' His second command, when it came, was the gospel. You never questioned that.

Then there was Sunday. Bed was nice; comics to read and books. My bad head used to come on at about ten o'clock, the tummy upset, the toothache, the forgotten homework, all frantic reasons why I should not go to Carmel, our chapel. My parents rarely went there, but we had to go; they saw that we went and saw that my sister, Gloria, who was about seven years older than Gethin and me, got the 'nippers' into Chapel. Life was Welsh in Gwaun-cae-Gurwen. Everyone spoke Welsh first and if necessary translated words into English for the benefit of any who could not understand. There were four or five chapels. Everyone belonged to one of them.

I would not say that I am religious in any deep way now, but from those days I have an in-built sense of guilt; a bit negative maybe but it helps me find a moral code. I have an immediate shudder if I blaspheme. I do a lot of shuddering on the rugby field!

Sermons in those days were always too deep for us. The boys used to take soccer diaries in to the pews, look at the pictures and pick their world teams. The Rev. Hughes would call us to our feet one by one in the morning service to recite out chosen texts. Gloria used to plan something ambitious for me and rehearse me on the way to chapel. Then when I was called, I would panic and trot out the same old line almost every time, '*Cenwch i'r Arglwydd ganiad newydd*' (Oh sing unto the Lord a new song).

'*Daiawn,* Gareth, *Daiawn,*' the Reverend Hughes would nod, appearing to give my regular message the concentration and acclaim of scriptures previously unheard.

The clock would drag its way up from 11.30 to 11.50 before – escape. Sunday lunch, as only Sunday lunch can be, and I would bleat from behind the tight collar of my Sunday best shirt and dark suit, 'Can we go out the back please Dad and have a kick about for five minutes.'

Whatever he said, we would go, but not for long, because it was time for Sunday School at 2.30.

Going to chapel got better and better mainly because as I got older the girls became more attractive. So, after

Sunday School we chatted them up and had a coffee; then, after the evening service, there was just time for another lightning coffee with lots of milk and a rush down the Falls for what we called a 'snog'. Then came a new minister, the Reverend Evans. He was a younger man who appeared to understand the tangles of youth. He talked football to us. He played soccer himself, and he fished too.

Of course I had to sit still in Chapel, and there was one other place too where the threat of 'captivity' loomed over me for a while – the brass band.

Gwaun-cae-Gurwen has a famous brass band, renowned at *Eisteddfodau*, pride of the village. One day, there it was, something small, compact and shining in my hand, my new companion . . . a cornet. What use was a cornet to an eleven year old who rarely stopped running long enough to draw enough breath for a dotted crotchet? There were musical traditions in the family; I suppose that was it. My father's father played in a big silver band up in Ammanford and they once played in front of the King at the Crystal Palace. He was one of seven brothers who were very well-known in local concerts as The Pencoeds (named after a street in Ammanford). So there was a bit of Edwards music history to pursue.

My Dad had no opportunity to play music himself but he went out of his way to help me, and it was his secret wish, without really pushing me, that I should report to the pub, the Mount, in the upstairs room, and blow a cornet. Reluctantly, twice a week, I used to go along for practice. Often I would rush down to band practice from the field and blow my cornet with the cold sweat running down the middle of my back.

I used to make all sorts of excuses at home to my mother to get me out of playing my scales and practising the third cornet parts. Eventually I hit on a winner. We had been advised by the band-master that spittle or mucus would collect in the valves of the instrument if we did not soak it in water from time to time. 'Gareth.

You haven't done your practice,' my mum would say.

'Duw, Mam, terrible cornet this. Full of mucus all the time. It's in the bath soaking.' My cornet spent so much time in the bath soaking it had almost mastered the breast-stroke by the end. Mam got wise to me and I remember the day that she made me practise up in my bedroom. The boys were playing up the field. It was a beautiful evening. I hurled my cornet on to the bed in frustration. It hit the spring mattress, shot up in the air, and then wallop – the floor tonked it. Flattened it was. The tone I blew with a proper cornet had been pretty frightening; now, with a bashed one, it was a disgusting mixture of wind and spit; not even the old faithfuls, the Christmas carols came out! That was it – the end. I rushed down to the pub with some raffle tickets we had been selling for the band outing, my money, and the cornet. Band practice was hours away; I made sure of that. I found Maggie, the landlady there, minding her own business, so I handed over the tickets and the cornet. 'Do me a favour, please,' I asked. 'Give these tickets and this cornet to the conductor. He knows about it.' Off I ran like a yearling who had once again beaten the bridle; off down the road and up to Archie's field.

By the time I was eleven or twelve, soccer was no longer a sissy's game. Lots of the lads had moved from the village school down to Pontardawe and had come back with talk of Swansea Town. We had always kicked a soccer ball around the street, but now everyone wanted a team. However, we had heard how the Cwmgors village boys played in a smart set of jerseys so we decided that we had to be like them.

Down we went to the local shop and bought up some old cloak-room tickets. Then we went to a farmer and got a cheap chicken. The vegetables came from our dads' gardens, so without much trouble we were launching a raffle for a chicken dinner.

It was a success, and days later we went down to Swansea on the bus and marched into Atkinsons the sports shop with £5 in our hands. 'Ten Manchester

United jerseys, please,' we asked.

After a search the assistant came back shaking his head. 'Only eight there boys, but you can have ten Arsenal shirts.'

'Who plays for Arsenal then?' Besh asked.

'Mel Charles does and Jack Kelsey,' I chipped in.

'Great club, the Arsenal,' whispered Ade, as if he was confiding some great secret in us.

But then the assistant made his first mistake. He lifted up a Manchester United jersey again and we ogled at it to see the new white V-neck and the trims on the sleeves. None of us had been anywhere near Old Trafford in body, but in the mind we had picked up the ball midfield, fed Duncan Edwards out on the right, raced on to the far post to take a nod down from . . . and driven the ball low into the corner of the net. These heroes may have died at Munich but they lived on as far as we were concerned.

In unison, 'We'll have the Manchester United please.'

'But what about the other two?' the assistant inquired.

'Let's have two Arsenal shirts,' Jeff said. 'We can pretend that Arsenal's full backs are on trial and we'll transfer them when some new jerseys come in.'

It was a great idea. The jerseys cost 9s. 6d. each, and here we had two First-Division full backs coming to play for Gwaun-cae-Gurwen colts on trial!

Of course in those days, there was no mini-rugby, no comprehensive school set-ups giving organized sport. The only organized game I played to the age of thirteen was a rugby match against Brynamman School. It was the greatest happening in our whole school life. I started off in the centre, but when we couldn't get any line-out ball I went in the second row . . . and then when we could not heel the ball I moved myself to hooker. But I fancied centre most.

We made up our own team when we were fifteen years old and just over. We used to charge off every

Saturday playing eighteen or nineteen games in a season. We were good but we were cocky. We beat
Brynamman 63–6, and when we were 21–nil ahead at
half-time in the return match they all walked off. We
were so full of ourselves that one day we decided to take
on Craig Cefnparc at soccer. They were a proper soccer
team but we could beat the world. We lost 27–1 and no
one mentioned soccer again for a long time.

I often wonder if our way of learning games then was
not better than today. If you spend your life kicking a
ball around the streets or a small field, then you acquire
a lot of ball skill. I do not want to come the 'old soldier',
but tackling bigger boys, often on the road, beating
another lad between the pavement and Mrs Davies's
wall, gives you a hard core of ability which comes second nature – a bit like Yorkshiremen playing cricket. I
am sure that the boys these days get more into the set
pattern play of rugby and perhaps can call moves which
are quite sophisticated, but have they got the skill with
the ball?

In Gwaun-cae-Gurwen and districts around, a
demi-god was a man who played for Cwmgors; a God
was a Cwmgors player who had had a game for
Swansea, Neath or Llanelli. Every Saturday was a
ritual. After I had played all the morning I would be off
with my 7d. to the chip shop to buy chips, rissoles and
pop. Then up to Cwmgors's field to stand on the touchline. 'Cum' on cherries,' everyone yelled. I can
remember, when Cwmgors had won, a very rare happening now I come to think about it, running through
the streets ahead of the triumphant players and telling
everyone, even if they were old ladies shopping who
didn't care if Cwmgors had won or lost. All I needed
was the Olympic flame in my hand. It was a serious
business to me, spreading the good news.

In the Swansea Valley, like all the Welsh valleys,
rugby interest was crystallized into a near-obsession.
Every Saturday morning there would be young men
and old standing on corners with duffle bags or boots

and towel, waiting for some broken-down team bus to pick them up to take them somewhere to play. The smells of wintergreen oil, dubbin on the ball, beer out of enamel jugs, and fish and chips too are the Saturday smells of a Welsh valley upbringing. Sadly I only played once for the 'cherry and whites'.

I wanted to be part of Cwmgors rugby so much. I wanted to be grown up. One Saturday, we young boys followed the Cwmgors team back from the field to the Welfare Hall where they had a shower. We hung around the changing-room, scraping mud off boots, handing in jerseys, anything to get in on the act, when suddenly I really felt I was one of them. I knew that I was going to take my clothes off and get in the shower with them. I whispered the dare to the other boys. Some agreed, and in we went like a flash, soaping down as if we had just played a West Wales cup-tie. It was great until one of the committee noticed us standing there knee-high to a second-row forward, and kicked us out. We had no towels. We just dressed again. 'Ullo Charlie,' I said to one of the most popular players.

'Mr Thomas to you boy,' he came back. Squashed. I remembered that for a long time afterwards.

There were three other important seeds sown before the age of fourteen when I moved out of Gwaun-cae-Gurwen during the day for schooling.

The headmaster of the Primary School was Mr Bryn Evans, a meticulous man in school, 'Who dropped that pencil?' or 'Who moved that chalk?', so many tiny points. Yet out of school hours you could see him disappear *draw'r wlad* (out to the country) towards the Black Mountains with his fishing rod. He used to come back late in the day with trout and salmon. I was at the stage when I used to tug out eels from the local river (full of coal). In later life he taught me fishing, which is now a great joy to me. Many years later this rather severe class-room figurehead would be asleep in his bed at six in the morning and I would have to wake him up by throwing stones at the window. We would cut sand-

wiches and set out *draw'r wlad*. Then in Welsh ...
'Come on, Gareth, I will take you to where there is a
pound of fish under every tree,' and we would set off
over the Black Mountain, the other side of the rainbow,
until the village, still sleeping, was far behind us.

The next was a rugby experience which no boy
forgets, his first sight of Wales at Cardiff Arms Park.
Huw Eic's dad was going to do a report on the radio for
BBC Wales after the game so he took us both up. I
remember it clearly; it was Dewi Bebb's first cap, England 1959, and Dewi became my personal hero from
then on because he scored the try which won the game,
5–nil to Wales, the very same try which I myself had
scored so many times up the field and in the square,
and which Huw had converted over the lamp-post.

We got to Cardiff Arms Park early, hours before
kick-off, so that we could get down the front, next to the
railings. It rained non-stop all day. The players were all
mud and we were soaked. There is not much about the
game I remember, but I do recall arriving at the BBC,
then in Park Place, and being confronted by the commissionaire who was looking at us very strangely indeed
when Huw asked if he could see his father. Not surprising either because Eic himself burst out laughing when
he came to the door. We had bought green and white
cardboard leeks to pin on to our red and white hats and
the rain had washed rivulets of green and white down
over our cheeks.

Anyway, fate is a funny thing: Dewi Bebb's last game
for Wales was against England at Cardiff in 1967. It
was my first in front of my home crowd.

My other taste of international rugby was the long
trip to Murrayfield by train. It was the cheapest way up
there and eight of us set off one morning, joining the
special train at Swansea which looped around the tiny
West Wales halts before going up to Crewe. Our
mothers were very concerned because we had little
money to buy food, so my mother came to the rescue.
She spent an hour cutting bread and cooking sausages

for us. 'Come whatever,' she lectured us. 'You'll not starve. That lot will see you through the whole weekend.'

The little train chugged away, picking up the locals every few minutes. One and a half hours later, we were still only in Pontardulais, about ten miles away from Swansea as the crow flies but by now eight juvenile bellies were bulging, jammed full of sausages and light ale. Not a morsel left and two days to go!

The third matter of importance which was growing was my relationship with a skinny girl in my class in the Secondary Modern School called Maureen Edwards. She was so thin, she was the only girl I knew who could walk through the school railings without drawing breath. She did not exactly rave about me. One day the physical education mistress told her that I would make a nice boy friend for her. She reacted to the news with some horror. 'Not that cocky little so-and-so . . . ,' she said. She saw nothing in me and the feeling was mutual. She only told me about those feelings when we married twelve years later.

So, equipped with an eye for fishing, rugby and gymnastics if not for music and Chapel, and taking a passing interest in girls, I felt that life was as full as could be. My Dad did not agree. One day he came into the kitchen, a solemn look on his face, and letting out a sigh, he dumped a miner's hat, a lamp and boots on the table.

'Whose are those, Dad?' I glanced up.

'Just come to fit you out for them,' he said, ''Cos learning's not for you, that's obvious.'

Education? He was right. I had forgotten all about that.

3

The helping hand

He was a magnificent-looking man in the eyes of a thirteen year old: tall, squarely made, a sports coat stretching over a full chest. From somewhere inside his fifteen
stone came a deep voice of authority. Bill Samuel lived
in Cwmgors, took us in the Youth Club, and taught
down at Pontardawe Technical College. 'Hear you're
coming to the Tech., boy,' he boomed at me one day.
'Looking forward to it?'

'Yes,' I assured him. Whatever I thought, he was not
the sort of man you disagreed with. Anyway, I was
escaping the threat of life underground.

When I got to the new school I could see straight
away how much I would like it. Sport was important.
We had to buy two rugby jerseys, one blue, one yellow,
as part of our uniform. I had never played properly
organized games before. It had always been a case of
'reds on this side, colours on the other'.

Bill Sam was to have an enormous effect on my life.
He was one of the 'old school'. If you came with a note
saying that you could not do gymnastics or games
because you had a bad chest, he would be unmoved; no
sympathy. If you said, 'Sir, I have just heard that I
have two months to live,' he would give you a hefty tap
on the shoulder and say, 'Never mind boy, get out there
and make the most of it!'

As a result, everyone felt that they had to do something, and Bill Sam found a sporting niche for all. He
made the fat boy welcome, and the weak boy. There

was a wide range of track and field events which could involve the whole school, even if they could not all take to rugby. As for me, he knew from home that I was probably the sporting ring-leader in G-c-G and was not prepared to let me have my head.

'What position do you want to play, Edwards?' he asked one day.

'Centre, sir,' I chirped back.

'Brylcream position that, boy! Brylcream on your hair, and hands in your pockets. No, not for you. You are a gymnast; I think you're a scrum-half.'

'I played there once at school,' I said eagerly.

'I'm looking at it this way boy. You want to play for the Swansea Valley Schoolboys don't you? Well, you'll never get in the centre because the other boys are too good for you.'

Squashed. It had been decided.

What a debt you owe to the teachers who direct you in many ways at that time of life! Yet, judged even against the selfless standards of the best masters, he was outstanding. Already, even then, Bill Sam had considered my rugby and my gymnastics deeply. Hazy plans for my future formed early in his mind. I was just whizzing about like a run-away train. Happily he manned the signal boxes at various turns to make sure that I did not fly off the rails.

Bill Samuel was concerned, I see now, not that I might have been conceited, but that I had the right standards in sport. He was ambitious for me. I often scored tries in school matches from seventy or eighty yards. 'Gareth Edwards,' would come the judgement, 'dull play that; carrying the ball in the wrong hand.' Or another time, when we had won the game and mine was the only name on the scoreboard, he would come out with, 'Might have put that outside half in hospital once, and you missed touch twice.'

Although the criticisms were extended over a long time, I always had that feeling that he had it in for me. He shattered me to such a point one day that I went home and cried and told my parents that I thought he disliked me.

I used to train hard; very hard indeed. A typical games lesson would be first some athletics, with me doing a bit of everything, then perhaps cricket for an hour. I was a fast bowler, what else? Charging into the crease for half an hour or so and then exhausted, get dressed to catch the bus home. The bus stop was a mile and a half from the school, so we had to find the strength to walk that far. One day I was just putting on my tie when Bill Sam came in. He looked around and pointed at me. 'Where d'y'think you are going then?'

''Ome, sir.'

'Out there you're going, 'round that track: six two-twenties, twenty-four seconds apiece.' That was heavy going for a little kid. When through, Bill Samuel would take me home afterwards in his little red mini. One sweltering hot day, I will never forget, he dropped me off at the top of the street. In fatigue, almost illness, I padded home, hitting the railings on the way.

I just made it to the bathroom in time to be sick. 'What's the matter?' my Mam was concerned. 'What's wrong with you?'

'It's that Bill Samuel,' I whispered back. 'All this training is killing me.'

In the winter it was rugby only in school, and we used to play some big schools. It was hard rugby, partly because the grammar school opposition were older boys and partly because it was the way rugby was and is played in those parts. I played in the Swansea Valley Under-fifteen side.

I had been a scrum-half since the age of fourteen. Well, there was no way that I could not be, once Bill Sam had told me so. Hour after hour, it seems now, he would make me bounce the ball off a stump of wood, collect it, and pass it out. It was a dive pass. All the great scrum-halves dived to pass the ball. Not many seasons later I discovered the tough truth that I was not a very skilful passer. It was all part of the shock of starting in Welsh club rugby and international trials.

Pontardawe Technical College did not have games every Saturday, but luckily the Grammar School asked me to turn out for them in the odd game. One of these was down at Gwendraith and all the boys could talk about on the bus on the way was one of their sixth-formers who had actually played for Llanelli. He was an outside-half, not very big and we marked him well all through the game. Even so, he won it for them with two penalties and a conversion. I never spoke to him myself. I found out his name though. It was Barry John.

Quite a lot of the boys played rugby for the school team on Saturday mornings and soccer for their local clubs in the afternoon. The days when soccer boys were second-raters up on *Cae Archie* were gone too. Colbren Rovers flourished. I was just sixteen years old when I was picked out for a trial at outside left with the West Wales Youth Soccer team. They were the under eighteens. I was disappointed not to be picked for the final trial against North Wales, but it wasn't the end of soccer for me. Trevor Morris, now the Secretary of the Welsh Football Association, was then the Manager of Swansea Town, and he came up to my house. 'I'm not interested in the Welsh Youth side. I want you to sign for me,' he said in Welsh. The fact that he spoke in Welsh clinched it as far as my grandmother was concerned. She was happy. Trevor told her that he would look after me. His was a good performance. I think he only knew about fifty Welsh words!

Off I went to Swansea a couple of times a week to train with the Swansea Youth and Trevor was persistent. Other clubs offered me trials, but my mother said that she wanted me to get my O-Levels first. I had only got two, but had come close enough with five others to give me hope if I tried again. So Trevor Morris asked me to sign provisionally. What should I do?

Meantime, towards the end of my days at Pontardawe Tech., that thin, dark-haired girl from Gwaun-cae-Gurwen, who once reckoned that she wouldn't pick me up, not even with a pitchfork, was looking a different girl, really good-looking. I got my friend to fix me up with a date: seven o'clock, Brynamman Hall. I was not normally allowed to go to the pictures on a weekday, but my mother allowed me to go on this occasion. I was back from school; the evening all planned, when a knock comes on the door at about twenty past four. Mat Cullen was there. Mat was an athletics fanatic; a middle-aged man who was coach, chairman and president it seemed to me, of all athletics in the Swansea Valley.

'Gareth, I've got this girl down in Clydach, next Welsh long-jump champion. Will you come down and demonstrate the hitch-kick?' What a time for that!

Down I went, because he said it would only be ten minutes with her. I did my stuff, but then Mat, who had taken me by car, told me to catch a bus back home. I was mad. I caught the last possible bus to Brynamman, and what a relief to see Maureen still there. I was late, but I still made my first official date, and sat in the cinema with my running spikes wrapped up in a towel. I said I was going away soon, and would she write to me.

'P'raps,' she said. That was all.

4

Away from Wales

I was going a long way away, or so it felt to me, to
Millfield School in Street, Somerset. Bill Sam had fixed
it; it was his plan, though, of course, my choice in the
end. He still makes me laugh when he talks about his
correspondence with Mr R. J. O. Meyer, the headmaster.

Just imagine a letter arriving on that lovely antique
desk in the Head's study of one of the most expensive
schools in England, announcing that the sports master
in Pontardawe Tech. understood that they gave sporting scholarships, and that he only mentions it because
he has a wizard of an athlete who has won the Welsh
Schools long-jump with 21 ft 6 in., hurdles, throws the
discus, pole vaults and plays rugby and soccer. Name of
Edwards.

'Dear Mr Samuel,' came the reply. 'I have to inform
you that we do not give sporting scholarships as such at
Millfield School, and by the way I have a twelve-year-
old boy from Brazil who jumps 25 ft.'

That was that. Twelve year olds jumping that distance! I wondered what sort of place it could be. However, unknown to me, Bill Sam persisted. I learned later
that about five or six letters were exchanged and that by
the end it was a case of 'Dear Bill' and 'Dear Jack'.
R. J. O. wanted to see me.

I shall never forget that first journey to Millfield. My
brother-in-law and my sister took me because they had
a decent sort of car, a Sunbeam Rapier. Bill Sam was

with us, of course, and I travelled alongside him in the
back swotting for my Welsh O-Levels. It was a long
drive in those days, up and around the mouth of the
River Severn to Gloucester. Just before we got to Street
we stopped in a lay-by for me to put on my Sunday suit.
Then, on and up the drive. I couldn't believe it. It was
nothing like any school I had seen before. Beautiful tall
trees lined the drive and ahead on the crest of the rise
stood the lovely old ivy-covered house I came to know
as School House. On either side of us were nissen huts,
and I never imagined that they were classrooms. The
sun was shining; it was a brilliant day. There was an
easy atmosphere about the place. The students looked
enviably confident and casual, because they belonged
and I did not. All around there were sporting activities
going on – tennis, golf, riding, hockey and later I
watched the students swimming. It was never-never
land as far as I was concerned.

After an interview on my own, 'Boss' Meyer led me
out of his study to join the others on the front side of
School House, over a tiny stone bridge which crossed an
open ditch, and on to grassy slopes. A tea-table was
laid; the butler brought some cake; my eye wandered
below to the pupils practising on the lovely pitch-and-
putt course and I was introduced to another boy who
was there for an interview. He was author Ian Flem-
ing's godson. All in all, the Edwards family were
definitely on best behaviour.

After a while Boss called me aside and walked me
down around the little greens to the chestnut trees
which sheltered the field. He talked to me as if I was
going to be there soon. He was a thin, gaunt but athletic man; quite eccentric so it turned out. I believe he
once bowled an orange instead of the ball in a first-class
cricket match for Somerset. A year later I learned just
how much he enjoyed strolling around the grounds,
perhaps feeding the ducks, and always carrying a golf
club. He would stop and say, 'I'll bet you boys two shillings that I can hit that tree with this golf ball. If I hit it

I'll have your pocket-money, and if you win . . . now let me think . . . I'll give you an afternoon in the sun.'

He could remember every boy and girl's Christian name, a thousand of them, their parents, aunts, uncles, the lot. Yet he always looked a scatterbrain. He was an important man in my life because he was Millfield and Millfield was important to me.

His last words to me on that interview day were delivered with a laugh as he shook my hand. 'Well what you must remember m'boy is that not every day here is a May day but it is a day for good things to happen. Come and join us in September.' I was in, and sure enough next autumn I was on the road from the Swansea Valley to Street once again.

Millfield was full of people with money, or talent, or both. I mixed with millionaires and sons of millionaires, and I lived in School House, up on the third floor. There were seven of us: Robin Balding, the younger brother of the racing trainers Ian and Toby, me, and five sons of millionaires. You can imagine the sight in the big field on prize day. It was a field full of Rolls Royces . . . and my Dad's Morris Cowley. Yes, he was proud of that.

I was nervous of these people because they talked confidently and clearly, while I felt very Welsh and uncertain for a while. Yet it was after my rugby had become a school talking-point that Boss Meyer stopped me one day and put on a stern face. 'Now then Gareth, don't you look down on these boys because they are not great rugby players . . . and don't let them look down on you because your father's a "miner".' Fair enough.

I was older than most starting off there, and I was a prefect. That authority and my sport gave me self-confidence, and this is mainly where the school had most effect on my education, and certainly on my rugby.

Those nissen huts were cold. We used to huddle around the old-fashioned stove in the middle. Nowadays they have replaced the huts with semi-permanent buildings, but then I can remember being so drunk with the fumes from the coke that I once fell asleep in the middle of a scripture lesson. Well, that was my story when the master woke me up saying, 'Not boring you, am I Gareth?'

We were in small groups, between three and eight in the class, and we had a small dining-room in School House, which was dark and panelled. Boss used to have dinner with us, and I cherish those chill cosy nights when he would get to his feet after grace had been said and announce, 'Right lads. Some people have earned you beer with your meal tonight.' It usually meant that the school rugby team had won, and the beer jug did a round.

I can look back with affection on every single thing that happened at Millfield, and it is funny now to think how mighty we sometimes considered ourselves. All part of the process, I suppose. There was the occasion when I went into the bathroom and found a bath already run. I did not know whose it was, but, as senior man, I knew I could take it over. I had one foot in the water when a tiny young fellow came in. He stared at me hard and spurted out, 'I say. That's my bath if you don't mind.'

'And who are you?' I asked.

'I am the Earl of Offaly,' he replied tartly.

'Well, I'm sorry son,' I came back, 'I'm the Lord of Gwaun-cae-Gurwen. You can have it when I've finished.'

There was another boy named Bamford. He was always in trouble. A square, bouncy fellow who had a flood of swear words for every situation but he said them with such style it never sounded like bad language. More often than not he had to report to the prefect's hut on defaulters' parade. 'Not you again, Bamford,' I used to say. 'Right. Go and pick up all the leaves off the drive, or, clear off and weed the cricket pitch. Do something useful! Come back in two hours.'

Once, in frustration I asked him what he wanted to

do when he grew up. 'A steady job for the bloody council,' he replied without hesitation.

Years later, I went with colleagues on a business trip
to Uttoxeter. The first man who met us said, 'You are
Gareth Edwards, aren't you? Mark is looking forward
very much to meeting you.' A short time later, I was led
through a foyer with marble floors, stuffed elephants,
just like a Hollywood set. It was a lush set-up. And
there he was, Mark Bamford, son of J. C. Bamford, of
JCB plant machinery fame. Not exactly working for the
council!

It was a fine reunion, and I was delighted to see that
the original Bamford spirit had not been crushed by his
lofty position. He confessed that his green Rolls Royce,
which incidentally, on that day, matched his suit, had
not yet been registered. It bore a trade number plate
which he wanted to keep for a while – 007. 'When I'm
in London,' he smiled, 'I've got 'em bloody well licked.
They don't know whether I am Sean Connery or Roger
Moore.'

What happened to my sport at Millfield was sudden
and spectacular. Perhaps I should emphasize that in
Pontardawe I had been an athlete first and a rugby
player second. I took great pride in my athletics, yet
within twelve months I was given a bit of a rude
awakening. In Wales I had been the bright boy as a low
hurdler but now I was moving to higher hurdles and
into competition which was rather hotter than I
expected. Nor did I ever seriously train for athletics.
During my first winter at Millfield I had been chosen to
play rugby for the Welsh Secondary Schools and there
was never any time to work at summer sports.

Anyway, like everyone else in that first summer I had
a tilt at the All England Schools Championships. That
was the top; two thousand schools competing first on a
County basis. So off I went to the Somerset meeting.

I was allowed just one event and chose the high hurdles – 3 ft 3 in. now, not 3 ft any longer. It was a typical
West Country field, all downhill, and bang! – away I

went for 120 yards winning it well in 15.1 seconds. I realized that in the conditions it was not a legitimate time, but balancing one thing against another and considering my lack of practice, I thought I would be able to improve on it in training.

The All England Schools Championships were at Watford that year, and to my eye they were organized as well as the Olympics. Certainly it had never been as impressive in Wales. I was first on. The gun went to open the games at 11 a.m., and 16.1 seconds later I was finished! Well beaten and a poor time as well. After that I always had that uneasy feeling that I was not growing as quickly as the hurdles. The Welsh fish was swimming for his life in a very big pond indeed.

Just a glance in school at the medals won by Mary Rand was enough either to inspire or depress. She was older than me and I was rather shy of her. The school always appeared to be having half-day holidays for her wonderful long-jumping achievements. Many years later, at an Open Day, I remember Boss Meyer joking to me, 'Just think if I could have got you and Mary together. God only knows what I could have produced.'

In my second and last year at Millfield I had at least worked out that low hurdles were better for me, and it was off to the All England Championships again, this time at Blackburn. The English record for the 200 yards low hurdles was 23.1 and there was a tremendous fuss when Graham Gower broke it in the first heat with 22.5 sec. I went off in the second. I can't ever have run better. Bang! 22.4 sec. Marvellous. Then came the semi-final and I won that too with 22.6. In the final Gower was ahead but I fought and fought and somehow got back to win by, dare I say it, a nose. We clocked the same time 22.5, a United Kingdom record.

During the next few hours one of the strangest feelings in sport came my way. I was picked to represent England! Yes, the England against whom Huw Eic and I had scored so many winning tries. Wooden spoonists of Colbren Square! Me playing for them? Unbelievable.

We were to run in the British Championships in Ireland and there was a tannoy announcement – 'All winners are to report to the organizer's room to discuss travel arrangements to Belfast.'

'Who's coming up from the south to catch the train at Crewe?' they said. I put up my hand.

'Where from?'

'Swansea, sir,' I said, and surprised the official who stared, coughed, cleared his throat and pressed on.

'Ah, yes. Crewe for you then.'

When the trip came I felt extremely lonely but I remember well how pleasant everyone was when I scrambled into the carriage at Crewe. Rosemary Stirling I recall particularly, though I do not think she will remember sitting near me. She was kind. Alan Pascoe was there, and so was John Davies, all British athletes in the making. We crossed to Ireland from Heysham and soon I was walking around the tartan track in my English tracksuit, the rose on my chest, with my father, my ever-supporting sister and brother-in-law at my side. I was proud. Odd to think now how many times since that uniform has been a red rose to a Welsh bull!

Even stranger, as the teams marched out, side by side, I was alongside two Welsh athletes, one a shot-putter and the other a sprinter, with whom I was destined to share many of Welsh rugby's greatest moments, Alan Martin and John J. Williams.

'Bloody traitor,' they joked.

'Hey,' I whispered, 'Gimme a lift home from Crewe.' When it was all over I duly returned with the Welsh tribe.

That is one part of life that gives me a thrill, to meet people who I knew when I was young who have really made the grade, at anything, not just sport. I like to remember them as they were. I hope people think like that about me, because it was not so long ago that I was with the boys in Gwaun-cae-Gurwen crowding around a Welsh Rugby Union handbook and saying, 'Duw! duw! How did Ken Jones get forty-four caps? He must have played for ever.'

Boss Meyer's attitude towards rugby football was simply that he wanted the school to be the best. There were two Welsh masters, Sid Hill and Herbie Davies. Sid was rotund, ginger hair, from Morriston near Swansea; and Herbie played for Pontypridd, so he said, and for Taunton and was younger, and a bit fitter than most in his Carnegie College blazer. They did an enormous amount for me, giving me confidence on and off the field and a very Welsh comfort in their houses. There is more than one side to the game and Millfield rounded me off. For example, Herbie and Sid would take us off to play in London or Paris or somewhere. We would finish the game and they would say, 'Right, chaps. The bus leaves at eight in the morning. You'd better be on it. Here's ten bob each and you can get a nice steak and a bottle of coke, or five pints of beer. Don't make fools of yourselves and don't let the school down.' Our games were reported in the *Daily Telegraph*, we were well-known players.

It was education of such a different sort from what had gone before. There were miserable moments of homesickness of course. Sid Hill used to ask me to his house to eat lava bread, Penclawdd cockles, and put on the London Welsh choral record of Five Thousand Welsh Voices. I suppose we felt worse after than before.

By we, I refer to my Welsh rugby friends Vaughan Williams and Nick Williams. Vaughan was from Barry, a tremendously talented outside half. Nick, who was later to be best man at my wedding, was from Newquay and had as strong a Welsh accent as mine. It was when we had travelled to Yorkshire on the train with the Welsh Secondary Schools side that he asked if I thought he would stand a chance of getting into Millfield. He did.

Nick had great trouble in speaking slowly enough for people to understand him in English at first, but he was none too accurate in Welsh either. I remember him coming to my house in Gwaun-cae-Gurwen. My mother opened the door.

'*Ble mae dy dyn di*, Mrs Edwards?' asked Nick.

'Oh Nick! Really. You are a silly boy,' my mother let him in and walked off.

Nick thought he was saying, 'How is your man, your husband, Mrs Edwards?' What he actually said was, 'How is your bottom, Mrs Edwards?'

Everyone who knows me realizes how happy and proud I am to be Welsh, and in those days away at school, it was natural that the Welsh should spend a lot of time together. What I have never believed in is the herding together of the Welsh on a Lions tour. We have had a bad reputation for being clannish, and on several overseas tours the team spirit has suffered for it. But on the British Lions tours I have made, it did not happen. That is as true of the defeated touring team in South Africa in 1968 as of the winning teams in 1971 and 1974.

Millfield was always in the rugby news. The fixtures were glamorous. We seemed to be up and down to London twice a week. Seven-a-side was a speciality and we vied with Llanelli. Joyce Meyer, Boss's wife, was as keen to know how the first team had got on as he was. She lived it, and had no choice sometimes. Often I was in the surgery with an injury to look at and she would put the lamp on it. She really cared. At one stage I was training so hard I felt tired all the time, and she said that fatigue was setting in. I turned up at the surgery absolutely white and she ordered, 'Off to bed. No lessons for you today.' She brought me lunch in bed, then tea, fresh fruit, ice-cream and all the goodies, and then told me I could go out for training for half an hour, no longer. So I did some light stuff on the tennis courts under the floodlights, and very soon she was packing me off to bed again.

It was all to play at Stradey Park against Llanelli Grammar School, one of the finest games, both sides unbeaten and a Llanelli ground record to capture. They had taken ours. The ball never stopped moving. We won 5–3 but if it had not been for exceptional tackling on both sides it could have been 55–53.

My game got better and better. I was capped twice for the Welsh Secondary Schools against Yorkshire and France in 1965, and when I got home Christmas time Bill Samuel was still at hand planning for me.

'Good thing for you to play for Swansea,' he had decided. 'I've written off to them.'

So he had, saying that one day I would play for Wales and that it would be a good idea if they gave me a game over Christmas. The reply came back that they weren't really interested because they had a boy called Euryn Lewis who had had a Welsh trial. It was more or less a case of, don't call us, we'll call you. Yet Swansea did come up with a game for me, against the UAU I think, but I had to write and tell them that I was under eighteen and too young to play in first-class rugby.

Anyway, I was delighted with Millfield. I lived for the rugby there. We had a phenomenal side, but Bill Sam kept on scheming. 'I think now that the club for you is Cardiff,' he announced.

Cardiff were a bit reluctant, but I managed to get into the third team playing half a game in the first trial. It was a dream performance, and in the car before going on the field Bill Samuel actually predicted it. Although I was only given a half he said, 'Bide your time today. They'll all be trying to rush about, but I promise you, there'll be a try on for you, from about the half-way. Wait for that then, all right.'

I waited and just on the half-hour there it was – a break on down the blind side. I punted the ball on, raced after it and got the try. When I was back in Millfield, tucked away in School House, and thoughts of Welsh rugby were far behind me, I received through the post the Cardiff Players' handbook. It was an imposing black and blue. Yes, I thought, it had to be Cardiff one day.

Then unfortunately, I had an injury in school which put me out until the spring term; not a very popular injury with Sid Hill either. He had begged me not to play soccer for the school one Wednesday, because we had a big rugby match on the Saturday. However, it was too much of a temptation for me in the end, because I was on that bus to Dartmouth before anyone had missed me. Not far into the game I got a crack on the ankle. I stayed on, even scoring two goals. The ankle began to throb on the bus and when I was dropped alone at the bottom of the school drive (as it happened the others were boarded in houses outside the actual school grounds) I just could not walk. I shouted with the pain, started limping but could not make it. I hopped on the good leg, but it was much too far to keep that up with such pain. The only course left was to commando-crawl on the grass verge. Eventually someone passed, saw me, and got help. Sid Hill, so I have heard since, refused to believe that I was out of Saturday's match until he went into an early lesson and saw me on crutches. He looked a broken man.

Not half as broken as I was, however, and by the time I was fit again the Welsh Secondary Schools had found a new and talented scrum-half, Selwyn Williams. Selwyn since then has had a marvellous career with Llanelli, and we have had some dogged battles.

I have the luxury in my own book of recalling just one story which tells of my affection for the Meyers. My leg had recovered and I was in demand again by the Welsh Secondary Schools as the trials approached for selection against England at Twickenham.

The consultant who had repaired my leg lived in Bristol, the father of one of the girls in the school, and I could never have made the journeys to see him if it had not been for Joyce Meyer. She used to drive me back and forth.

We were chatting on the way home one day, both happy that I was in the clear; 'signed off' as they say at home. Quite off the cuff she put to me one of the most important questions of my life. 'Will you now be playing for the Welsh schools at Twickenham, or for the

School in the Roehampton Sevens?'

I replied by instinct, and sometimes that is best, 'What would *you* like me to do?'

'I'd love to win at Roehampton,' she said quickly, almost under her breath.

'Right,' I said, 'I'll play for the School.'

It was her wish without actually saying it, I knew that. I told Wales I was not available, though I did not know whether I would be selected or not.

At Roehampton I kicked goal after goal, I could have been blindfold and they still would have gone over. I was top scorer in the competition. We were accused of being professional, as Llanelli had been in previous years, because we slowed the game down. We had enormous press coverage for three days and we won a magnificent final against Whitgift. I hope it doesn't sound conceited. It was just a great schoolboy moment.

We had a night out in London; no doubt there was beer with supper in School House and other houses that night, and I like to think that Joyce Meyer had a sip for me. I certainly had one or two for her.

I don't know what they were making of me at home at this stage. I was walking around Gwaun-cae-Gurwen uttering foreign sounds like 'ectually' and 'railly' bringing a frown of disbelief to Maureen's face. 'And where did you get that coat from?' she asked me one summer's night.

I gave her a stare; undid the double-breasted buttons, opened it up, and snatched a quick glance at the inside pocket. Fortified, I then stuck out my chest like Napoleon and declared 'Harrods, in fact,' – not too familiar a name in the Swansea Valley. But you must admit, it would have been rude at school to say no when someone offered you a coat which had gone out of fashion!

5

Quite a year

From a boy I knew that the men who opened the doors to paradise and gave away Welsh jerseys were called the Big Five. What power! They control every Welshman's dream of running out at Cardiff Arms Park with the Prince of Wales feathers on his chest. If you have never been capped, selectors are gods, and I can remember talking about them in whispers with other hopefuls in the Cardiff College of Education. The sight of a selector at a College match early in the 1966 season, my first term at college, was greeted with excited mumblings on the field.

Mr Glyn Morgan puffed his pipe on the touchline and nodded occasionally. Welsh selectors are good at agreeing with everybody and then doing something different. There were five games ahead – Australia were touring before Christmas and afterwards came the four home countries in the New Year.

This particular College match was against Cross Keys. Mr Morgan was thought to have come to see John Jeffrey play. He was an outstanding number eight, and everyone said that he must be near a cap. I just played like hell and kept a conceited eye on the sidelines to see if he was still there. But it was all easily solved when some spoil-sport pointed out that Mr Morgan's son, Geraint, was playing for us. Nepotism is not exactly unheard of in the politics of Welsh rugby selection and of course there will always be stories of favouritism. I remember the Welsh hooker of later days

Jeff Young being very sensitive about talk that he was only in the Welsh team because his uncle, Jack Young, was a selector. Jeff was very much a players' player and he would always have been in my side when he was fit and well, but it was some time before he was able to ignore the typical Welsh gossip about back-stage corruption.

Imagine the shock when I was showering and Geraint Morgan came up to me. 'Hey Gareth, my Dad says you'll get a trial if you keep on playing.'

What would you make of that? I certainly did not intend to retire at the age of nineteen; I was rugby-mad. My club was going to be Cardiff and I had made my first-team debut before September was out. I started in the famous Rags, the second team, in a game at Briton Ferry. Next there was a visit to the Memorial Ground to play Bristol United and finally, I shall never forget the day I achieved my ambition of the moment, to wear the Cambridge blue and black of Cardiff's first team. It was against Coventry at Cardiff, a home debut.

What a wonderful atmosphere in that club-house afterwards. The supporters always crowd in for a pint; the club has a huge following. It was full of great rugby names. In the team itself were Keith Rowlands, the captain, Howard Norris, Billy Thomas, Bill Hullin, Maurice Richards and Ken Jones, all international players in their day. Then, with a half of shandy in my hand, and, I suppose, my mouth open watching this new, exciting world go by, I saw Bleddyn Williams. I thought of my first meeting with him about six months earlier. I felt a bit embarrassed now because I thought he might remember how naïve I had been then.

It was when I had been chosen for the Welsh Secondary Schools at centre to play against England. Selwyn Williams was scrum-half. The game was in April and I went to the Cardiff club just before that with Bill Samuel. 'There's Bleddyn Williams over there. Go on m'boy, go and ask him if he's got any tips to give you about playing centre. Tell him you are in the Welsh side next week.' So instructed, I went across to the great man.

Bleddyn was kind. He talked about getting your first tackle in, about getting an early feel of the ball, and made as much sense as he could to a scrum-half who wanted to be converted into a centre in five minutes.

Eventually I was spared the job of playing centre in that match because it snowed and the game was off, but I just wondered if Bleddyn knew that the Cardiff scrum-half that day was the student centre of some months back. He did. 'Where are you going to turn up next?' he asked.

'I'm staying put now,' I replied. A few months later I was running out onto the field in Cardiff colours as full back!

The year ahead had everything – promise, contradiction, happiness and deep disappointment, recognition by the Welsh selectors and rejection. It was a helterskelter of twists, turns and surprises.

First of all, Mr Morgan, the selector, was as good as his word. Across the Cardiff Arms Park one evening, into a training session, ran John Huw Williams, a former member of the College and a Cardiff player himself. 'Well done, Gar. You're in the Probables. It's you and Dai Watkins against Alan Lewis and Barry John.'

Well, that was something – half a miracle at least – a Welsh trial.

The Australian tourists were in the country struggling to keep their heads above water, especially in the mid-week matches. They lost to Eastern Counties and also to Cardiff in a match where there was one outstanding hero, Bill Hullin. Bill was Cardiff's vice-captain and after that game I saw him as a stong contender for the Welsh scrum-half position as well as a club-mate.

The day of the trial came, 12 November. All the interest in Welsh rugby turned to an unlikely venue, Maesteg. It is not a very grand ground. There is always a warm welcome in the club-house and the Maesteg side have had their good years too, but this was hardly a preparation for an international experience on the field. The pitch is high up on a hill, exposed and windy. The turf on this occasion was uneven and the rain continued where it had left off the night before – a constant downpour. Nowadays with a national stadium available it is so much better preparation for players to play trials in the surroundings and on the surface where they will play the big matches.

Anyway, back in 1966, in that dark dressing-room I changed quietly in the corner. I inhaled the sweat and the wintergreen of my heroes. Dewi Bebb was there, David Watkins, Denzil Williams and the two Brians, Price and Thomas. I saw the muscle, bone and the jutting jaw of Aberavon's loose forward Omri Jones . . . and was glad he was on my side.

I only knew two players, Ken Braddock and Dennis Hughes, the Newbridge back-row men. When the teams had been announced the Newbridge coach asked me over the telephone if I would take a trip up to their ground to work out some moves with his boys. I did, but the training lights were like a couple of candles on tripods. *Now,* I nodded to them uncertainly; I just presumed they were the ghostly figures who had been through those rehearsals with me.

Just think of the modern trial by comparison. The whole concept has changed, though I am delighted to have played through the transition. What the introduction of coaching and the international squad system brought to Wales was not just greater efficiency. Its introduction coincided with some gifted runners like Gerald Davies, J. P. R. Williams, Barry John, Phil Bennett and J. J. Williams, and I should add John Taylor to those. To get the natural skills from these the balance of the side had to be right. John Dawes at that time, never struck me as being an international-class centre, and indeed his particular art, of setting up the runners with a half gap and perfectly timed pass, could rarely find expression in trial matches such as the

Maesteg game. Later, watching Ray Gravell thump his way through the midfield, or Steve Fenwick generally dipping into the action now and again, did not persuade the selectors to say, 'We must have them in our side.' It was simply a matter of those skills being required to release the runners. Gravell's talents in defence were vital, and his particular asset of physical strength was used to set up second-phase ball. Fenwick, in his turn, possessed a Dawes-like sense of where to be and what to do with the ball at any particular time. So out of deeper thought and more intensive planning came a near-professional game, but still a sport and a spectacle which thrilled the players as much as the spectators. What was hard to assess was how vital were the players of real talent. Would it fall apart without them? There was a feeling that the method alone would carry the team through. In many ways I sensed a decline of individual skills.

With the thought and outstanding runners came the most brilliant of the arts, the counter-attack. Great tries have now been immortalized on television videotape like the one which I had the privilege of rounding off with a dive to the corner against the All Blacks at Cardiff Arms Park for the Barbarians in 1973. Phil Bennett started that off, just as he was the one to score the try against Scotland at Murrayfield in 1977 after Steve Fenwick had sent Gerald Davies sprinting out of defence near the Welsh line. Who did what in these tries does not truthfully matter. They just demonstrate an attitude of mind; a realization that an open space is an open space inside one's own 25 as well as outside it. At Maesteg on that wet Saturday in 1966, it would have been called recklessness.

The Probables lost; that was bad enough. Even worse, the press were very critical of my service and my feeding of the ball into the scrum. It was true. No one could say that I had a bad game, but in those two respects the comments were fair. At least I can see that now, even though I used to protest as hard as I could.

I was uncertain, though I was sure too, that I was good enough. I am still left with nightmare memories of my hooker Jeff Young, having his first chance to displace Norman Gale who was injured, glaring at me from the ground. Yet another scrummage had broken up on my put-in with the referee pointing a penalty to the Possibles! I got so tense in the end my hands gripped the ball like shells stuck to a rock. I just could not let it go, so that by the time it actually went into the scrum the tunnel had collapsed in agonies of anticipation.

What about the pass? It was short and erratic to David Watkins, and the fear of never being chosen again used to flash through my mind in those days, and that never helped. Alan Lewis was selected to play against Australia, as everyone had expected, me included, because he was a current British Lion, just returned from New Zealand that summer.

There was one newspaper comment which gave me hope. I cannot explain just how much. It sounds silly now after fifty-three caps to say that a couple of comments scrambled down the telephone to Fleet Street on that rainy day in Maesteg had a bearing on my career, but they did.

You see they were written by Cliff Morgan. 'Young Edwards may not win his first cap this time, but I predict he will win dozens before he is finished.'

I cut it out and studied it over and over. If the great Cliff Morgan believed that, then I must be good enough. Those were my thoughts.

My relationship with Cliff ever since that day has been warm. We always have a couple of drinks together when we have the chance, and I can remember the day that he even gave me a present of a suit. It was at the end of the Lions tour to South Africa in 1968. We were both homesick by then and glad to be thinking of going home. Cliff remembered that I had fancied his suit; the smartest I had seen. He presented it to me just before he left, cleaned and good as new.

However, it was the first kindness, the generous write-up when I needed it badly, that I will remember most.

The events which follow are fascinating to recall because no one could possibly have written such a script of surprises for Welsh rugby in one season.

First of all, Australia beat Wales at Cardiff Arms Park. Now how could that happen? Alun Pask was the Welsh captain and he was surrounded by British Lions and men of experience. Australia had proved by now that they could field one reasonable international side but, mid-week, they were below that standard. They had no depth and no form.

Consequently the reaction of the Welsh selectors was savage. British Lion Hadyn Morgan was never seen on the international field again. John Dawes was sent back to London Welsh for a two-year exile. Delme Thomas and Denzil Williams went out for three games. However, Gareth Edwards profited from the slaughter and got his card, again for the Probables, to play the next trial at Swansea – the final trial.

Now what was I going to do about that pass? Swallowing all the pride of a Millfield 'star', and in my heart of hearts knowing that I was a much better passer than I had looked, I picked up a telephone and got through to a Carmarthen number, the Training College in fact, because that was where the new Welsh outside-half lived. His name was Barry John, my partner in the trial.

Barry's first cap had been against Australia, so I thought that he would be keen to show everyone that he was a good enough player. On the telephone he sounded easy-going and said that if I turned up at college on Sunday morning he would take a ball out with me. So down I went to the West, and after a bit of a search I found his accommodation block. I climbed the stairs, knocked on the door and went in to find him lying on his bed, looking rough and unshaven, tired out by a party the night before. His room was untidy. He was not my picture of a Welsh outside-half. He looked more like one of the Great Train robbers hiding out!

The truth was, he had forgotten about the practice and even worse he could not remember where he had left his boots. I was immaculate in my Cardiff College track-suit, polished boots, all fresh and clean and my outside-half wore an old T-shirt, gym shorts and gym shoes which, on a wet sludge of a pitch, were going to be about as useful as wellies with holes in them. But I was anxious and mumbled, 'I might not have the best pass in the world but I reckon I can get the ball out to you from almost any place. How d'you want it?'

Then came the immortal words. 'Gar, you just throw it, OK, an' I'll catch it.'

That was the B. J. plan, so obvious that it worked. Mind you, that was his philosophy about everything. He had this marvellous easiness in the mind, reducing problems to their simplest form, backing his own talent all the time. One success on the field bred another and soon he gave off a cool superiority which spread to others in his side. Physically he was perfectly made for the job, good and strong from the hips down and firm but slender from the waist to the shoulders. However, on that day in Carmarthen he was on his backside most of the time, sliding all over the place, but I got my first whiff of relaxation from him and I felt better for it.

So, on 21 January, it was Probables versus Possibles again. Up went Brian Price in the first line-out, down at the Mumbles end. It was perfect possession and I sent out my usual dive-pass with my heart thumping and a prayer on the ball. Even before I hit the ground I said to myself, 'Thank you God.' I knew it was a good one, and when I looked up Barry was off in full flight in a lovely wide arc around their back row. It was too good to last. Crunch, came the tackle; the butterfly had been swatted. B. J. had gashed his knee severely and was carried off after only three minutes play. David Watkins switched from the Possibles. He was very understanding and stayed nice and close. The passing was adequate.

What about my other problem, putting the ball into the scrum? Norman Gale was the Probables hooker this time. I had seen off Jeff Young! Brian Rees was in the Possibles.

Norman had heard of my troubles and he obviously did not mean to go the same way as Jeff. 'Cum 'ere,' he said in his gruff way. 'Look, I know the referee Dai Hughes. He's an old pal. I don't care how you put the ball into the scrum as long as you put it under my feet. We'll be all right. He's told me.'

First scrum – whistle. 'Penalty. Not straight Reds.'

Second Scrum – whistle. 'Penalty. Feet up Reds.'

Third scrum – whistle. 'Penalty. Not straight Reds.'

At the fourth attempt to obey the instructions of Wales's senior hooker, Dai Hughes took me aside. 'Once more in crooked lad and I'll send you off.'

Big Norm raised his head from the front row and mumbled, 'Oh cum'on Dai, give us a bleedin' chance.'

Norman got the same. 'Quiet Norman, or you'll go off as well.'

There ended the old pals' act.

I was taken to Scotland as reserve for the first match of the home international season. My early hunch was right that Billy Hullin would figure in the selectors' plans. He was chosen for the first time. Nothing went right for them there, and I learned that however much you want your country to play well, there is no way you want them to win if you are a travelling reserve. They lost by 11 points to 5.

It was the first time I had ever flown. It was the first time I had been part of a senior international match too and I gathered more experience and determination from the dressing-room that day than from all the advice and trials that had gone before. I saw those Prince of Wales feathers on the red jerseys stretching over the chests of the chosen few and knew that I would give my life for one now that I had got so close.

You can imagine the disillusionment then when the team for the next game came out, and Alan Lewis was chosen scrum-half with Gwilym Treharne of London Welsh reserve to travel. No Hullin ever again, and Edwards, it had been decided, so I discovered years later, would be better left until next season. As if to rub it in, the Welsh team came to practise on the College ground and I could actually see them from the window. I watched Alan Lewis pass. I remember saying to myself, 'Yes. He's got a great pass. They've got the right bloke there.'

Wales lost to Ireland at Cardiff 3–nil, good stuff for a reserve to bite on. Trouble was, I was no longer heir apparent. I felt a reject now, and that I had been as near as I would ever come. When Selector Cliff Jones turned up to watch a College game against St Paul's College, Cheltenham, I was then certain that John Jeffrey was close to getting in.

On the evening that the Wales team to meet France in Paris was announced I was walking along the corridor of the Training College where there was a telephone. I said to a pal of mine casually that we could find out the team if we rang the *Western Mail*. Within a minute his mouth had dropped open, his thumb was cocked half in the air and he literally spluttered, 'Hey, it's you. You're bloody well in against France.' He put the phone down and laughed out loud, but I couldn't join in. He must have it wrong. Perhaps I was reserve again; perhaps they had given him the team upside down.

'Ring again in a different voice,' I asked.

He did, croaking away in a posh accent. The scrum-half for Paris was indeed Gareth Edwards. 'C'mon, we're down the pub to tell the lads,' he shouted. Off we went.

I think we must have been the only people in Cardiff who did not know that I had been chosen. The lads, seven pints to the wind, cheered me in, and I warmed to my new role by ordering orange squash, just to show them that my dedication had begun. After all it was nearly time to phone up another fly-half and ask him to cope with the Edwards pass. It was to be David Watkins, the team captain.

Only now, in the seventies, when team preparation is so sophisticated, I see what a Steptoe outfit Welsh international rugby used to be. Finding out if you were picked was torture because you always had to scramble around for the news yourself. Mind you, even these days things go wrong. I think of the Irish game in Cardiff in 1977. The team was chosen on a Thursday early in January and, according to the new system, the players chosen would get two brown envelopes on the Friday morning, one invite for squad training and another for the official match selection. I was a bit impatient on the Thursday night and I rang the selector with whom I had a special relationship, Clive Rowlands. Was I going to get my forty-fifth cap?

'Tell me the team, Clive,' I said (in Welsh of course).

'No, not even to you,' he came back at me. 'You'll find out in the morning.'

'Come on mun, Clive. Am I in?'

'Look Gar, I am sworn not to tell, and I am not going to. You'll hear in the morning.'

But Clive, who recognized the anxiety of not knowing from his own playing days, was moved to suggest, 'Look Gareth, how many changes do you think there have been since last time?'

'I reckon three of four in the pack and Burcher for Gravell, 'cos he's injured, in the centre, and I think Phil is captain.'

Clive chuckled and replied in his brusque way, 'Now, I haven't told you a thing, have I Gareth?'

'No.'

'I hope you get everything right on the day too. So go to sleep good boy and relax. Tarra.'

Next morning only one envelope came through the letterbox. It was an invite to the squad practice at the Afan Lido, but I knew the team, and did not worry that the official match invite was not there. Just before going to work I gave Phil Bennett a ring, quite early to congratulate him on being captain for the first time. '*Llon-gyfarchiadau*, Phil. Congrats and all the best. I hope it's a happy one.'

Phil sounded strangely unexcited by it all as we bab-bled on for a while. As we rang off he said, 'Well, happy New Year to you Gar. Thanks for calling.'

'Hang on, Phil,' I shouted. 'You know why I am ring-ing, don't you?'

'Well no, not really. I thought you just wanted to wish me a happy New Year because I'm not in the side for the Irish game. I've only got a squad letter this time. Who are you playing with, John Bevan?'

'*Myn uffern i*, Phil,' I laughed. 'You're captain. That's why I'm ringing. I haven't had two letters either.'

It is hard to describe a joyful silence, but that is how it sounded to me. It says a lot about the uncertainty of international sport that although you can be in brilliant form, as Phil was, you are still haunted by it.

Anyway, there were two minds at rest and we were spared one thing – by 1977 I had long given up tele-phoning fly-halves begging them to try out my pass.

Back to 1967 and the magic day drew near. Immedi-ately, I felt the weight of the vast Welsh rugby public. From the moment my mate put the telephone down in that quiet College corridor I said goodbye to my pri-vacy for ten years. The congrats, the back-slapping, the criticisms, the invitations, the cameras, the microphones and all that a great but greedy rugby country feeds on, were released like a giant waterfall on top of me. In those days before my first cap I was flattered when camera crews followed me along the touchlines and reporters queued to talk to my Mam in her spotless kitchen. I suppose it is all part of the business of being a top-class sportsman, but there were to be times when I could have put everyone, the lot, up against the wall and blown them up. Instead I turned to the family or sneaked off to fish one of my favourite rivers.

David Watkins and I had a practice which, even by the standards of those days, was comical. We met at the Cardiff Arms Park on the Thursday; the team were flying to Paris the next day. We could not find a ball for a long time, until the groundsman gave us a Cardiff practice ball. Nor did we change our clothes. We just slipped off our jackets and tossed the ball about in our flannels and ordinary shoes in front of an audience of two – our girl friends! David said, 'Keep the pass short so that you feel safe and you'll be all right,' and that concluded the private practice for Paris. The team then went through the motions of rehearsal on the Friday in Paris itself.

I thought there were a lot of television cameras and reporters in Wales, but it was nothing to the performance of the French press. At our run-out they were almost on the field playing with us they got so close. Leather-coated interviewers had an interpreter under every armpit so when you said, *'Non parlais Français,'* they launched one at you.

The Hôtel Normandie, one of the great hotels, had virtually been taken over by the Welsh Union and hangers-on. The huge open lounge in the centre of the hotel looked like some very lush waiting-room, and Welsh fans flooded in and out, pressing into the small bar, some a bit the worse for wear, claiming distant family connections with most of the players before asking for tickets for the game. Generally the noise, the chatter of Welsh, English and French, the sniffs of garlic and French cigarettes made a big build-up for the next day, 1 April.

For me the morning was full of people, impatience and anxiety, though I never for a moment thought I would play badly. A trip had come across from Cwmgors, travelling all night by boat. They were exhausted. First thing in the morning I gave my bed up to my auntie for her to rest and Besh, one of the boys, had been sick over his coat so I loaned him my blazer for the day. My Mam and Dad were there and of course my sister and her husband.

Anyone who played at the old Stade Colombes will remember the sensation of running out from that dungeon of a dressing-room below ground and jogging up and out into the sunshine. My boots gleamed, cleaned by my Dad, and the crowd roared the loudest roar I had ever heard.

I do not remember much about the game. I played tidily enough, and I remember when I got that first ball and I kicked well, the big boys Brian Price and Denzil Williams said an encouraging, 'Well done!' We led 14–10 at one stage but eventually lost 20–14. It was the experience which has stayed with me rather than the score. Up through the long dark tunnel, into the Parisian sunlight, the whistles, chants and roars. I was nineteen and I had made it. I kept looking down at the three feathers. They were mine. Only for the prophet Bill Samuel was this the end of the beginning. He saw more to come. For me it was the ultimate.

There is nothing quite like a fine French team romping around. We lost all right, 20–14, but we were still slightly disappointed. Although we had gone there to be slaughtered, so everyone said, we had not done too badly. As I came off weak with the feeling of having got that Welsh cap out of my system and almost deaf with the shouting and whistling which had gone on for eighty minutes, I felt a touch on the shoulder. Dewi Bebb stood there 'pregnant' with the match-ball under his jersey. 'That's yours,' he said. It was like giving me a bag of gold.

Stuart Watkins was next to come to me. 'I think you should get the French jersey today,' he said, 'we'll try to work it out.'

He went across and asked Darrouy. He should have had a few French jerseys at home because he played for France ten years before. I should add quickly that I was not going to give up my Welsh shirt but Stuart offered to hand over his. I could hardly believe that he and Dewi could think of a newcomer so much.

Darrouy unfortunately said that he did not want a Welsh jersey. He had enough of them. However he did tell Stuart that if I went back to his hotel afterwards he would give me a French jersey there. I followed him all over Paris, I think. I never let him out of my sight. Just imagine that beautiful gold badge on that lovely blue jersey. It had always seemed a million miles away when I was watching in the crowd. In exchange Darrouy wanted a Cardiff jersey and I sent it as soon as I got home. My retreat from Paris was complete, barring the lost match. At least I had the ball and two international jerseys more than I had when I went out there.

When I played in Paris in later days my heart still beat fast.

Yet, as the years passed, the knowledge of what was ahead of me at the end of that dressing-room tunnel was a help. The experience paid off. When the anthems were played on future occasions I could swell my chest, take in the whole atmosphere, notice things in the crowd, feel that it was a privilege to be out there and, most important of all, think. You can't buy experience they all say.

Anyway, in this unpredictable season of 1966–7, there were still other experiences to come. Three of us were new caps, Ron Jones, Dai Morris and I, but there were other novices in Paris who had had their first cap in the last three matches of that season – Bill Raybould, Gerald Davies, Brian Rees, Bill Mainwaring and John Taylor. How should we behave in Paris? The older brigade were clearly set for a night out *extraordinaire* and appeared to know all the haunts of previous trips. They were *formidable*, Terry Price, Stuart Watkins, Dewi Bebb, David Watkins, Denzil Williams, John Lloyd and Brian Price. Brian Thomas was a reserve.

The official dinner afterwards was so grand. There were fourteen courses, I am sure, and all that wine! I sat with Gerald Davies, two new boys who had not tasted life like this in Kidwelly or Gwaun-cae-Gurwen. The meal had started, then suddenly, with a clatter, they arrive – the Welsh Foreign Legion. Monsieurs Brian Price, Denzil Williams, Brian Thomas with a few side-kicks trailing behind including Terry Price. They had been having a 'few jars'. They approached like millionaires bursting out of their dress shirts.

Our circular table was now full and the meal went on with splendid style until – crash! I was surely in the middle of a bomb! The lights went out, there was another bang, and loud roars of laughter. To this day Gerald and I never found out exactly what happened. All I know is, that when the lights came back on we were sitting, as isolated as we had been before, but with no table, no friends, no nothing. The 'Legion' had vanished.

I learned another sporting lesson that night; the sadder side of the game. I saw the end of a great player in the candlelight of a bar in the Pigalle. Terry Price was a truly gifted player, and the Welsh public had raised him to the level of a star. But that greedy public hate being let down by their gods, and Terry had come in for more and more abuse as his game went through a bad patch. That day in Paris he had kicked poorly, looked slow about the field and never had a single stroke of luck either.

He had been struggling back after a cartilage operation. He should never have been passed fit to join the Lions in New Zealand during the previous summer. When he arrived out there, no one could believe the shape of his knee or the bulk of weight he had put on while he was at Leicester University. At his home nothing went too smoothly either. His was a hard upbringing in Hendy near Llanelli.

In Paris he was a shadow of that confident goalkicker who sent the ball revolving majestically towards the posts, or the natural ball player, strong, clever and elusive.

But that is how I intend to remember him. Forty-five points in eight matches for Wales before he went off to Rugby League for £10000 later in July.

In the Pigalle we sat it out in the bleary hours of early morning. He ordered a bottle of wine from the barmaid. She passed it over. Terry smiled at her. 'You remember me, Monsieur Price? Last time we have wine on the house.' '*Ah oui*, Monsieur Price. Very well I remember, but not this time. This time Terry Price, *il est fini*.' We laughed and paid up. The truth was blurred but it was the truth nevertheless.

The sad end of Terry Price, who was duly dropped, was the beginning of another brief meteor, Keith Jarrett. What a match that was, Jarrett's match. I was picked, but the selection of this eighteen year old took lots of the attention from me. I was now a veteran of one game. England planned huge celebrations down at Cardiff. After all they only had to beat a bag o'nails to win the triple crown.

Newport had experimented with Jarrett, normally a centre, at full back in their club match on the weekend before. He was so disastrous they swapped him around at half-time. Anyway the selectors shocked everyone and we took the field in beautiful dry, sunny April weather. The pitch was hard mud, but nothing in the elements of pitch conditions was going to change a game that was surely predestined – for Keith Jarrett.

The first time he touched the ball he kicked it over the sticks off an upright. The second time he found the middle, and the only kick at goal he missed all afternoon was a narrow-angled one which hit the post.

The fairy story was complete when he picked up a loose clearance by McFadyean and raced down the left touch for a try in the corner. England had been 15–19 down. Now they were further adrift, and when young Jarrett turned around and banged over the conversion from the touchline – well, that was too much for everyone. It ended 34–21 to Wales. Keith got 19 points himself. I remember poor Phil Judd, the English captain, at the dinner saying, 'We scored 21 points at Cardiff and lost. I just don't bluddewell believe it.'

There was just one more hint to the future of Welsh

rugby which came out of that lovely sunny day. The reserve outside-half Barry John, in a chat with Gerald Davies and me, said the he would not mind moving from Llanelli to Cardiff because he was certain to get a job there when he left College that summer. By the next September he was in blue and black, and that was going to be important to us.

However, the year's experiences were not complete, because Cardiff chose me to tour South Africa as reserve scrum-half to Bill Hullin, who was the captain now that Keith Rowlands had broken his leg and retired. I played full-back occasionally. New sights, new grounds, amazingly generous hospitality, wonderful fun with the boys, all these were injected into my system and until the day I retired it has been the pattern of my life. If I could ever pay back a hundredth of the treats and kindnesses done me in an international rugby-playing life which included three Lions tours, tours with Wales and with Cardiff, then I would be exhausted and penniless. Perhaps this is the moment in the book to say to everyone in the world who has entertained me a sincere and honest thank you.

With Cardiff in South Africa I was very much the junior, careful of what I said, and sticking a little to John Huw Williams and Gerald who were from my part of the world. I learned what it was like to go short of oxygen on the field, how to behave at lunch with Dr Vorster the Prime Minister, and how to accept the word of a pilot if he tells you that Dakotas will get off the ground, even though they are crammed with old bus seats and our heavy team kit! The engine spluttered, the oil flew out from all sorts of rivets on the wings and the only player oblivious to fear was a large forward who had had his drinks doctored by one of the lads. He had never touched brandy in his life, but beer after beer went down with the secret lacing of brandy in them. The effect was disastrous. The whole brandy bottle was secretly emptied. We arrived at Upington, and he was legless. The welcoming party were out on the tarmac, what should we do with him?

One sage suggested that we put him in the team's kit basket. In the end we carried him quietly away, out of sight as an advance party went out to chat up the hosts. But we had to come clean; he looked terrible. By chance, one of the hosts was a doctor. He examined him, looked up sombrely and announced, 'Poor chap. Can't travel very well. What he needs first is a couple of tots of brandy!'

I saw for the first time South African forward power, yet listened to Hannes Marais say that we had 'not always played in the true spirit of rugby, but in the spirit of the moment. You are a dirty side.' I watched from full back one of the greatest Cardiff performances ever when we beat Eastern Province 34–9. I saw that Maurice Richards on the Cardiff left wing was a fantastic player. When he wanted to play, no one stopped him. He never drank, smoked or swore and was known to be a religious boy, but he had a streak of ruthless determination on the field which made him superb.

Another Cardiff back, rich in talent and fun, was Ken Jones, or 'D. K.' as he was known. He had been regularly in the Welsh team since 1962 and had been to South Africa before, with the 1964 British Lions. He was a natural player, classic sidestep and a true burst of speed. His solid hips bounced off many a tackler and if his own tackling was somewhat irregular on occasions, his attacking skills more than made up for the odd enemy whom he took ten yards to pull down by his sleeve!

What Ken had inside him too, was a streak of individuality which made him reject the introduction of compulsory squad practices which were starting up in most clubs. Roy Bish, the Cardiff College lecturer, whom I still reverently called Mr Bish until he told me to drop it, was one of the first coaches analysing everything, and taking it very seriously. How could Ken Jones, bursting with the true amateur spirit, accept it? He would often run the warming-up laps and with a wave of the hand disappear down the tunnel off to the showers with a, 'Sorry Roy, can't stay. Little meeting on tonight.'

In one of the build-up sessions before a match in rainy Cardiff, the coach gave the order, 'Right, down on your backs.'

Ken took one look at the soaking wet, muddy field and just stood there. 'Look, if you want to get pleurisy, you get down, but I'm staying where I am.'

Even in a tight and tense game in South Africa in front of a big crowd he was heard to say to his fly-half, 'Kick it down to the twenty-five, on the right. There's a lovely looking bird down there.'

Yes, not for D. K. was rugby re-routed to near-professionalism. It was not that he thought nothing of planning and rehearsal, it was just that he knew it was not the whole of his life, and I respected him for that.

Roy Bish was my College lecturer. In contact with him daily and most evenings, I learned to think about rugby in a constructive way. He drew attention to patterns of play rather than to any techniques at that stage, and I became most friendly with him and his wife Annie.

So the young Edwards observed and inwardly digested. The battle now was to keep my place at the top, because on the horizon were black storm clouds which were big enough to test anyone's ability at the top. The New Zealanders were about to set off for Britain.

6

Making the grade

There is something about the blackness of an All Black jersey which sends a shudder through your heart. Fifteen of them look dark and sinful; eight snorting bulls and seven black panthers. It takes a second or two to tell yourself that they are only human. It takes a success or two of your own before you know they are saying the same about you. I simply stood and stared in the autumn of 1967.

Yet perhaps the colour does betray their attitude to rugby football. It is hard as flint. They are raised as boys to compete and no preparation of the mind or body is too tough. The game is part of their body and bone. No one teaches them about failure.

Wales mustered its own conceit in 1967 as never before. We have a lot to be proud of in our rugby, I know, but, in these days just before coaching took a strong hold on our game, we tended to believe that the patron saint of rugby football was Welsh and that he would protect us from defeat and make us brilliant in victory. I am sure that the Welsh Selectors did not think that. They were hypnotized by the size of the challenge to seek out the biggest forwards in the land.

I was twenty years old. The fables about the past and all the great New Zealand players intimidated me, but on the side-lines all the time was Bill Sam, still prompting, 'C'mon my boy.'

It was to be a short All Black tour before Christmas. 'A good game against them,' announced Bill Sam, 'and you'll be regular in that Welsh side and then it's South Africa for you, with the Lions next summer.'

There was sense in what he said, I realized that, but I could never bring myself to speak the words 'British Lions' to anyone. I remember being afraid of the opportunity and kept on reminding myself that I had played only two internationals.

That was an awkward term in College as well. One minute I was driving into the Cardiff club-house, everything about it like Manchester United, the big time. Next I was getting my backside kicked on a muddy field such as Bargoed, with the proverbial man and dog watching. I felt I wanted to do the right thing by the College as well as Cardiff. I had loyalties in both directions, but I was often torn between the ideals and worried myself unnecessarily. However, I was never again as fit in my life. I trained with the College on Mondays, with Cardiff on Tuesdays, Wednesday was match-day with one or the other; then training again on Thursday, and Friday off. On Sunday we often had squad practice with the Welsh team, and so all the rugby and the daily gymnastics left me too tired for anything else. I don't look back on it as a sacrifice, though I can remember wanting to go for a pint with the lads more than once instead of running around, but honestly, I wonder how I did it for so long.

The All Blacks began their campaign at the White City, Manchester, by beating the North of England 33–3 and on they rolled over the Midlands and Home Counties, the South of England and England itself at Twickenham 23–11. The next match was at Swansea. West Wales were captained by the old fox Clive Rowlands, and I was watching with the 42000 as he gave the All Blacks a really tricky day. He reduced the lineouts to a couple of men and whenever he could, kept the ball ahead of his pack with those kicks into the box or high down the middle. New Zealand eventually won because Graham Thorne, in the centre, raced right though the middle from his own half and scored under the posts. It ended up 21–14 to the All Blacks. The next game was against Wales.

I was sure I would be selected because I had been asked to captain the East Wales squad in preparation for their game against the tourists a month later, in December. I had never thought that I would be made captain, though I already had confidence in my ability, and therefore thought I could do it. Wales were looking for someone at that time who could inspire, because apart from that win over England we were erratic.

Both John Jeffrey and I were chosen for the Welsh match, and we were comforted by the sight of West Wales doing so well at Swansea. I remember seeing the great Colin Meads in action there at St Helens and being amazed that he was not ten feet tall with one eye in the middle of his forehead! He was much smaller than my nightmares had told me.

Saturday, 11 November came, and it was a ghastly day of high winds and pouring rain. Norman Gale was the Welsh captain and he prowled around the dressing-rooms like a caged bear. We had that jumbo pack which the Welsh Selectors had clearly set out to recruit. Brian Thomas was a prop with Denzil Williams. The Aberavon boys Max Wiltshire and Billy Mainwaring were in the second row and Dennis Hughes, the Newbridge number eight was moved to the flank to allow John Jeffrey in, with John Taylor on the other side. There was inexperience too. Behind the scrum there were first caps for Paul Wheeler at full back, Ian Hall in the centre and Keri Jones on the wing, and at forward for Jeffrey, Wiltshire and Hughes.

As far as Norman Gale was concerned the whole game rested on the first scrummage. 'Anyone not with me in that first scrummage, I'll kick his arse around the Arms Park for the rest of the afternoon.' Coaching theories had arrived, just, but now the old grit and thunder was back again. If there was a real fear, it was not physical, but we knew we could lose to New Zealand even if we played very well. I remember feeling that we were not looking past that first scrum. If we failed there, what the hell were we going to do next?

When it came, I remember the scrum so clearly. It was towards the town end of the ground under the South Stand. The packs retreated fifteen yards and sized each other up, and with yah! ugh! and a crunch of shoulders they made contact. I had never before seen anything like it. It was the psychological moment, the test of will and it really did feel as if that was the match over. The referee's whistle went. 'Get up, get up,' he choked. I looked at him; he had gone white. He tried to be authoritarian but his voice was cracked and nervous. 'Don't go down like that again or I'll penalize someone.' They broke up, turned and looked at him, then . . . boof . . . down they went again.

Only fleeting memories of the game survive. I remember the second after my first pass to Barry John. Tremain came down on my arm and jammed it. It was as if I had sent my jersey to the laundry press forgetting to take my arm out first. The pain went all up my back. If the ground had not been so wet and soggy he would have broken it. A huge contusion came up on it, with stud marks. It must have been accidental, I thought. Surely no international player would ever do anything dirty; this game was surely the ultimate in talent; they didn't need to play any tricks like that. I soon learned better, but I do remember picking myself up and running off in agony, telling myself again that it was an accident. I looked at Tremain more carefully at the next line-out. There he was, seventeen stone, playing as a wing forward. He had had a cortisone injection in order to play so I knew he must be pretty important. He was massive; ears on him like hydrofoils!

After going down under a ruck, the other flank forward, Graham Williams, rolled over close to me, close enough to talk. He grabbed my shirt and pulled me towards him, just underneath him. 'Get under there, kid, and keep your head in or you'll get hurt.' He was right; the All Black rucking machine was like some giant combine harvester. Bodies were booted around like chaff and left in a space behind the pack along with the ball for Chris Laidlaw to sort out. Great gesture that of Graham Williams. I remember Laidlaw's pass. I admired it, quick and low and spinning accurately through the air. I soon skipped that stage too, thank goodness, of noticing what opposing scrum-halves are up to.

I kicked a high up-and-under, which was our main tactic late in the game. I followed and tackled Ian Mackae and cut his eye open with my head. Later, at the dinner I apologized and he said it was OK. The blood was dripping down his dinner suit, but they had beaten Wales 13–6 and they were happy. It was then that they revealed themselves as a great set of lads. We had a wonderful night and the rest is a bit blurred.

A month later I was facing New Zealand again but now as captain of East Wales. It was to be a remarkable game and, I promise you, it started from modest beginnings. The squad coach was David Hayward the old Cardiff and Wales forward. We decided to meet in the Cockney Pride pub to discuss our tactics over a curry. Conversation went like this.

'Got any plans, Gar?' said Dai, taking out a large sheet of paper and a pen.

'Well, we've only got one practice session, Dai, it seems a bit late to me, doesn't it for you?'

Dai chewed on his curry and sipped a drink quietly, his face dark and concerned. Then he calmly put the top back on his pen, folded the paper and put it in his pocket. His face brightened and a great smile came on his face. He had seen some great light. 'Yes, Gareth, we're going out there to tackle everything black that moves, to grab every loose ball we can find, run it and have a bluddy good go.' That was it. The East Wales tactics wrapped up in a sentence. Everyone now recalls it as the match of the tour. We ran them all over the field. Mr Saxton, the New Zealand manager, said afterwards that this was the fastest and best game of the whole tour. The All Blacks hardly got out of their own half. It was 3–3 in the end and even now I can see Barry John's final fling, a brilliant drop at goal from the left touchline, up to his ankles in mud, and he let fly . . . it's going . . . it's going . . . it shaved outside the post, and the draw had to be accepted. The East Wales backs were superb.

I missed a very kickable penalty that day and it dawned on me suddenly, now that I was captain, that you don't get two chances.

In retrospect, I do not think that twenty year olds, as I was then, should be given the captaincy at all. There was far too much onus on me and not just on the field. I was too concerned about what senior players in my side were thinking about me. Are the old campaigners talking behind my back? Do they think I am any good? Nowadays it is a different matter. For instance there was far less pressure on later captains of Wales with the backing of the squad system and a national coach than on me when I was first tossed into the job as a player with a few caps.

What I do remember of that East Wales match was the great night afterwards, even though I was worried about my first speech. Guess who had written me a few notes? Bill Sam of course, coaching and cajoling from the shadows. 'Listen to me, *bach*,' he said. 'If the All Blacks win you can tell them the Welsh proverb about the farmers, because they are a country of farmers. "In the field of the bad farmer there are many holes," and then you can say, "So there can be no bad farmers in your side." Then if you win *bach*, it is easy. All you've got to do is stand up, cry, and sit down again.'

Yes, Bill was always somewhere near me. He knew what it was like for me to play against the All Blacks as captain and have to think about speeches at the age of twenty.

Bill anticipated everything. Even later, as recently as the Lions tour of 1977 when Brynmor Williams was injured and Doug Morgan was carrying on solo, Bill

Need I say more?

Bill Samuel's fledglings. (End of front row, left.)

Price of Gwaun-cae-Gurwen County Primary. Edwards senior, back row extreme left; brother Gethin on the left on floor.

Specialists in Sevens. Millfield School, Spring Term 1965.
Standing – Mr Sid Hill, Louis Bush, Mike Dolding, Ian
Cattanach, Mr Herbie Davies. Sitting – Vaughan Williams,
Varnie Dennis, Andy Higginson, Gareth Edwards.
Trophies. Oxford (runners-up); Senior (Somerset); Llanelli;
Clifton.

First Welsh cap at Stade Colombes.
Standing – John Taylor, John Lloyd, Stuart Watkins, Dai
Morris, Denzil Williams, Brian Price, David Watkins
(captain), Bill Mainwaring, Ron Jones, Terry Price.
In front – Brian Rees, Bill Raybould, Gareth Edwards,
Gerald Davies, Dewi Bebb.

'Dawe de Villiers, neat and competitive, had all the attributes of a Test scrum-half.' One of our early meetings; the second Test match on the British Lions tour of South Africa in 1968.

Piet Greyling of South Africa with a few options available against Gwent, 1969–70. 'Greyling the destroyer, was one of the best flankers I ever played against.'

Sometimes Barry John appeared to wear a halo!

The familiar story . . . Mervyn Davies picks up the Welsh heel,
Edwards moves wide to support . . .

'You just throw it, O.K., an' I'll catch it.' The moment arrives for Barry John to keep his promise.

Great friend and foe, Roger Young of Ireland, on the break against Wales. (March 1971.) Mike Hipwell looking to support, and I am just looking!

Above: The protectors –
John Taylor, Mervyn
Davies, Sandy Carmichael,
Delme Thomas, Willie
John McBride, John
Pullin – without whom
nothing would be
possible.

Right: 'Will there be
another Gerald Davies?'

The 1971 Lions cannot lose the rubber to New Zealand now.
Colin Meads drinks a beer with us after the third Test.
John Dawes (no. 13), Barry John, John Bevan, Delme Thomas,
Willie John McBride, Gordon Brown, Derek Quinnell.

A welcome in the hillsides worth waiting for. Back from New
Zealand with honours, and the streets were lined from Neath to
the top of the valley.

Sam rang me. He felt my dilemma when asked to help them out. Are you going out there, Gareth? He saw the carrot as always — Edwards, the saviour, going out to rescue the beleaguered Lions, and help them win the last two Tests so clinching the series. Then retire. That was Bill's idea; go out in a blaze, beat 'em single handed like Roy of the Rovers. All I could see when the Lions management asked me to fly out to New Zealand was the feeling of stepping off that plane, overweight and bogged down with my own fitness problems. I had too much respect for the boys I was playing with and against, and for myself, to attempt the impossible, however glossy the dream might have been. Bill Sam was then happy when I explained my feelings. Right, he declared yet again, because he rarely conversed, only stated indisputable facts – 'It's the fiftieth cap . . . serve Cardiff and Wales for one more season, right through mind you, and then . . . it is finished.'

We went to the Cardiff railway station to see the All Blacks safely on their way to London for the final match of the tour against the Barbarians at Twickenham. 'See you on Saturday, boys,' I was able to say, as if I had played at Twickenham a hundred times. This was my first really big match in London but there were five of us from Cardiff in the side, Keri Jones, Gerald Davies, Barry John, Howard Norris and me. Max Wiltshire, the Aberavon forward was with us. Safety in numbers and what turned out to be a trip to remember.

The Barbarian officials had written to us to say that we were not staying in their usual hotel in Park Lane, but in a place called the Carlton Towers. 'It's not in Piccadilly,' said Barry. 'Can't be any good. It's in a place called Knightsbridge.'

We were told we could go up on Thursday, although the official team gathering was not until mid-day on Friday. Howard could not get away but we young teachers and student teachers, Gerald, Barry, Keri and I, duly set off by train on Thursday. It was so exciting. It was the first time we had ever set off for a game of rugby two days before! None of that Saturday morning dash.

However, before we had got to Swindon we were arguing who would pay for the taxi at the other end. 'They'll charge you the world up here,' said Keri with a tone of voice suggesting that if we pooled everything we had it would only get us a hundred yards. When we got to Paddington we panicked and settled for the tube. We jammed up the traffic at the underground map, four of us checking and double checking that Knightsbridge was a possibility on the Bakerloo line, and if not where did we change?

We came up in Knightsbridge near Harrods and asked where the Carlton Towers were, or was, whichever way you had to say it. All we knew was that it was probably a grotty place, because, as the Babas had written, they could not get into their usual accommodation. I can just see us, the four lads from the valleys, suitcases in our hands, walking down the road towards this tall hotel, but then, seeing the commissionaire, the fella with the ole top hat and uniform outside, we all instinctively looked at the ground or across to the other side of the road, whispering, 'Darro, it can't be that. It's far too posh.' On we walked, asking again two-hundred yards on. We were directed back and then we knew the smart place was ours.

I do not know what they made of Gwaun-cae-Gurwen, Kidwelly, Cefneithen and Ystalyfera at reception? We each pushed somebody else forward to sign the forms first. £15 a night it said – a fortune in those days! We giggled in the lift. The rooms were sumptuous. I rushed from lounge, to bathroom to the bedroom. 'Hey Barry. What d'y'think. There's television in every room, even the bathroom.' We leapt across the corridor to see if the other boys had the same. Yes, it was all too much. This was great, and all free . . . 'at least it is, isn't it, boys?'

Insecurity was not far away. 'I wonder how much dinner costs here?' asked Gerald.

'Do we pay?' I asked.

'Better eat something cheap,' said Keri, 'in case we only get a couple of quid allowance.'

Barry's contribution was to point out, as we walked into the restaurant that 'one dinner here is a week's wages'.

So we chose the cheapest steaks and signed the bill but made sure that if the worst came to the worst we could pay it if we had to ... but we would have to go carefully. It was only Thursday.

When Geoffrey Windsor Lewis, the secretary, arrived on Friday we were secure at last. Have what you like boys and sign the bill. The Barbarians are paying this one. The English boys somehow have more confidence than we do. There they were ordering veal *à la* this an' that, and even then, when we had been given the all clear, we could only bring ourselves to order a slightly larger steak. We couldn't even spend somebody else's money. We did learn that before the end of our careers!

Max Wiltshire managed to be a bit more daring, but by accident. He reckoned on match days that he played best on curry for breakfast. I remember him carrying a packet of Vesta curry with him in case he had to make his own. Anyway he tested the kitchen of the Carlton Towers that Saturday by requesting curry for breakfast in his room. They could not commit themselves: they would have to ring him back. So they did, inquiring, 'Would you be happy with a salmon curry, Sir?'

'Well, if that's all you've got,' mumbled Max. 'Ay. Bring it up. Thanks a lot.'

The salmon curry arrived with the bill to be signed for £8. Now that is one helluva breakfast by 1967 standards.

Let me just end my story of nervous beginnings up to the days of certainty by recording a few flashes of memory ... like seeing Waka Nathan racing past me on that afternoon at Twickenham, or Colin Meads running at me as if I was not there. I hung on to one of Meads's ankles and he eventually dropped in front of Barry, a debt Barry later acknowledged though I don't think he can ever buy me enough pints to pay me the true reward . . . of the hard game against England at Twickenham. We were hammered at forward but managed to draw 11–11. I got my first try for Wales. It was from a scrum in an attacking position five yards out. I went around the blind side after Norman Gale had taken a heel against the head. Great place to do that. I half-dummied and dived between two English players. Seeing that white line underneath me was a great feeling. I smiled too, on the way back to join the team for the conversion because I honestly thought of my brother Gethin and just how many tries we had scored for Wales against England around the blind side in Gwaun-cae-Gurwen . . .

. . . of the day I was chosen to captain Wales for the next match against Scotland at Cardiff. I was in the Royal Hotel in Cardiff. Immediately my apprehension returned of having to captain a side which included old hands like Brian Thomas, Denzil Williams, Norman Gale and the rest. However, the team chosen was young. There had been six changes. The only happiness came from the thought that I must be that much closer to a Lions tour. Surely the four international captains must go to South Africa.

By the end of the season there were so many captains it was impossible to apply that rule.

. . . of beating Scotland in a bad game on a bright day. Keri Jones scoring the only try after a forward pass. Wales did well enough but Edwards 'has to improve his passing', wrote the sages. Next game John Dawes was captain in Ireland. I did not feel at all disappointed that I had lost the captaincy. In fact the only time I did was the last time. Playing for Wales was the main objective in my life.

. . . of an Irish game which was a shambles. I dropped at goal and it was adjudged over by the referee but not by the crowd. People came onto the field throwing orange peel and bottles. A Guinness bottle hit me and a couple of pennies. Everyone was going crazy. The game from then on was full of incidents, but two wrongs made a right this time, because Mike Gibson dropped a goal which was touched in flight but still awarded. Ireland won. The mistakes were genuinely made by Mike Titcomb, a referee who was as good as any. It was just one of those things. It could have happened to anyone.

. . . of the match at Cardiff against France and a change of captaincy. G. O. Edwards was in charge again and it was afterwards mentioned in despatches that, 'Gareth Edwards has given a more accurate service than in previous games but Barry John kicked poorly.' Well, you can't win 'em all. France beat us and only the Lions selection now meant anything to the individual players. How did I measure up against Redwood and Pickering, Hastie, McCrae and Connell, Young, Quirke and Sherry? At least Wales had only picked one scrum-half.

7

The widening vision

In South Africa, that summer, life could not have been sweeter. I even got fourteen shillings a day to spend: more than I had ever had at home or at college.

Looking back now, the disappointments are gone, especially the depression about injuries. The record book tells me that I was having a successful tour, my style of play well-suited to the conditions, but there is no injury to destroy like a torn hamstring. I played the first two Tests but the tour was soon over for me, and I watched the Lions go down bravely 11–6 at Cape Town and 19–6 at Johannesburg.

There endeth the statistics, because this book is simply one of reflection and reminiscence. All that comes back to me now is the fun, the warmth of the sun, the dazzling hospitality, the long hours of leisure in a lovely country. If anyone had drawn a cartoon of me on that trip it would have portrayed a little dark-haired fellow, wide-eyed, bringing up a nosy but respectful rear to the old campaigners, Tom Kiernan, Willie John McBride, Syd Millar and the rest.

Touring is a great privilege. Even when the weather goes against you as it did for the 1977 Lions in New Zealand, or up on the High Veld where rugby at altitude makes you feel as if you are trying to gulp your way out of a hot oven, you have to remind yourself of one basic, self-imposed law . . . that it is a privilege to be travelling in someone else's country. Understand their outlook on life and you will enjoy yourself. Put *your* likes and dislikes on to your host and you will be a burden for them.

Having said that in all sincerity, I will now tell you that the '68 Lions were the greatest pranksters I have ever seen. It was almost expected of rugby players in those days that they would retreat to the dormitory days of their youth, sing bawdy songs and drink pints of beer. They were amateurs. Television had not yet reduced them completely to public property. Most people at home hoped that we would win but I think they were more concerned about our preserving the attacking traditions of the Lions. We specialized still, as a nation, in being good losers, but that was just about to change.

I remember we were given cigarette lighters as presents. They were the first free gifts we had ever had, and we decided to celebrate by burning everything. One day Tom Kiernan, the captain, was reading his paper at the airport when one of the boys set it alight. Next, Willie John and Syd Millar were sitting around on the patio of the hotel one night, and began fooling around. In the end, Willie ripped Syd's shirt. That was no good to Syd, so he turned around and tore Willie's and when he had got hold of it, set it on fire with his lighter.

I was with some of the other lads, watching all this from a window above. It was in the best of spirits and I promise you, the moment was right for a laugh. We had had some hard rugby and travel. I was a youngster there, but I did not think it was irresponsible. It was just high jinks.

I have since discovered that it is straight Irish logic, that if you loose your own shirt then no one else has a right to be wearing one, and very soon an ever-increasing band of shirtless bandits lay in wait for more unsuspecting prey. I remember poor old Pat Marshall of the *Daily Express* coming out of the hotel. Whoosh! Off came his shirt; the best advert for Oxfam I've ever seen with his white chest, thin ribs and braces.

But ah! Who approaches next? It was the hotel receptionist; good-looking girl, too. They told her that they wanted her pants to go on the bonfire. Not a sign of panic. She did not shout, run or anything; not a word. She simply walked smartly off to the bushes, returned holding her pants between her thumb and index finger with the dignity of the squire's lady at a coffee morning, wrist cocked and little finger crooked. The boys watched her drop that briefest part of her wardrobe onto our bonfire. 'Will that do?' She slayed us. They thought she would be absolutely demoralized.

Without a doubt it had the makings of the best bonfire since Guy Fawkes, then suddenly, without warning, a sheet of water passed us on the way down from the fifth floor. Someone had tipped a bucketful, but instead of damping the fire, it landed on Willie and Syd. They were so mad. They looked up and saw us ogling out of windows and thought we had thrown it. We were so scared, we ran and hid in cupboards to get out of their way.

Readers may be surprised by the schoolboy fear, but you must remember how young some of us were and also that this was the tour of the famous 'Wreckers'. I think the Wreckers were formed on the night of the train journey up the Kruger Park. It was such a long journey and obviously some of the lads wanted to go to bed. But the whisper was out, 'Don't go to bed, or the Wreckers will have you.'

You can imagine the experience of lying on your bed in total darkness, the train, old and magnificent like the Orient Express, steaming its way through the middle of the Veld, and suddenly you pick up the faint chant of voices getting louder and louder, 'The Wreckers are coming hurrah, hurrah.' By the time the crescendo has built up you are dragging wardrobes against the door and scrummaging against them as if you are trying to stop a pushover try in a Test match.

In the end I found it was better to join them than not, though there was a pacifist alternative founded by Bob Hiller called the 'Kippers', meaning those who intended to sleep without disturbance.

The Wreckers always worked out their plans in about two seconds flat. Perhaps after a few drinks around the pool, someone would say with a flash that I then thought was quite brilliant, but now recognise as rather uninspired, 'Let's go and get him out of bed,' or 'Let's throw him in the pool.' Once we stormed in to the wrong cabin and turfed a complete stranger out of bed. Luckily it was taken in good part.

At the end of three and a half months there was a famous, unofficial Lions' Court case to try for high treason two players who had never wrecked a thing, Maurice Richards and Keri Jones. The regular Justice, his Honour John 'Tess' O'Shea, had great deliberations with the prosecuting counsel before the two were found guilty. They were sentenced to perform an act of deliberate wreckage nominated by the judge. I can't recall what Keri had to do, but I remember Maurice first refusing, then carrying out an order to pick up a bottle and throw it against the wall. Everyone ducked, but as if by some stroke of invisible defiance against the verdict, the bottle bounced back off the wall unbroken. Maurice had triumphed. Next throw he smashed it to smithereens, but he felt that his little miracle had proved the moral point.

The playing side, as I say, was a bit of a disappointment to me because I got injured. It was even more annoying because I felt I was learning all the time. Tom Kiernan was a very wise 'old man'. Bob Hiller was playing well and kicking lots of points, but Tom fought off the challenge. He was knowledgeable and very popular.

The hard grounds and the rare atmosphere were almost unreal. Yet I instinctively took to it all; it was very much my game on top of the ground. I was too much of an individual – I can see it now – but had I stayed fit enough to play the second two Tests I think I could have benefitted more.

I appreciated other people's talents for the first time.

I suppose it was a product of the security one felt as a Lion on tour that one looked more towards the team's success. Victories meant happiness too, good team spirit, and respect from the South Africans. Mike Gibson was superb. He gave me confidence in my passing, because it was not as simple as playing with Barry John. Mike and I had first to understand each other's mental approach to the game. He had poise and judgement and was always thinking of the partnership and how we fitted into the whole back line. What I took for granted then, but I can see more clearly now, is his class.

Then again, it was the first time I knew for certain that Barry John was destined to be great. Someone said once that I could find him in a dark room. I could. It was more the feel of the partnership that kept us together, not codewords or pre-arranged plans. I could be under pressure, not able to see Barry at all, and throw the ball out into space. Somehow he nearly always got there and that gave me pleasure as well as confidence.

It may surprise rugby supporters to hear me talk of confidence as a Lion, but in the back of the mind there still lurked that skeleton of the erratic pass. Often the old headlines used to come to mind, 'Edwards must improve his passing.' I arrived at Eastbourne to join the 1968 Lions with an image of a new pass in my mind – Chris Laidlaw's spin-pass, which I intended to take into my own game. I told Barry John straight away that I would only dive-pass if I was too pressed to spin it, and of course he did not worry. However, he found it was good. He could take it easily and it gave him much more room than before. What a devastating blow it was for our partnership when he was carried off with a broken collarbone in the first Test at Pretoria.

Let me write the final word on my passing, because we have arrived at the moment of solution. I never ever thought about it again.

I was lucky because spin-passing came easy. I did not

really have to adjust. It was simply a question of body awareness and repetition. How can I ever regret those days in the gymnasium with Bill Samuel or in the Cardiff College of Education? Many critics have pointed out that I do not spin-pass out of my left hand, and I have thought over the years that I wish I had time to develop it more. I can pass that way but only do it when I have to. It was much easier for me to alter my feet position, to get my bottom tucked into the line-out and half-turn. I think it is advantageous to be able to spin the ball both ways, but I don't personally feel that I have lost anything by not doing it. It all boils down to one arm being stronger than the other. Out there in South Africa the ball travelled more or less in a straight line; not much deviation. Up on the High Veld, in that rare atmosphere, it went much further, but back at sea level we simply adjusted to a shorter carry. However, by the end of the tour it was near perfection. When I got back to Wales there was virtually never a word written against my passing ever again.

The Lions experience is a step ahead of home international rugby. You have more wise men around you; no one is distracted from the game; you learn to play with judgement more than pure emotion, though I must admit that nobody is as emotionally roused to the cause before a big game than I am.

For example, when the Lions played their first Test in South Africa in 1974, I was able to say to the new boys, 'Look, I remember we were in exactly the same position in 1968. When we run onto the field you'll hear the most deafening roar in the world. It will hit you straight in the face and go right to your knees. But when the Boks run out, it'll be like an atomic explosion. You'll feel like fainting. You will wonder if you can ever beat them. We can. We are better equipped; we have the ability and belief. Say that to yourself when they run out. Get them down to their true size, otherwise they'll be all over us. Remember the planning and the coaching, and stick to the methods you know.'

I know it sounds like a bit of a sermon now, but I am sure it was and is true. The quicker in an international career a player can detach himself from all that tiring emotion and calculate his game, the better. At the end of my career I may not have been so dashing a player, partly because I was always heavily marked, but also because I found that remote platform to stand on, to look and assess the situations as they arose. Well, most of them anyway.

A large part of the success of the Lions tour of 1971 was the presence of players who had been on that '68 tour. It is a credit to Tommy Kiernan and Ronnie Dawson that a lot of players learned a lot of things.

One Springbok stood above all others for me, Frik du Preez. He was a tremendous footballer. He could side-step and swerve like a six-foot Gerald Davies. My admiration for him was immense. If only for one try he will be immortal. He broke, all sixteen stone of him, around the front of a line-out and ran fully thirty yards, going around Tom Kiernan with amazing speed, to touch down without anyone getting near him at all. I can't think of any forward in my career who could have done that.

That was in the first Test in 1968 in Pretoria. Sadly my admiration for du Preez was then shattered in the second Test, which we managed to draw 6–6. Mike Gibson was pinned by his shoulder in the scrum formation; only his head stuck out. Du Preez roared in and punched Gibson with an almighty smash. It was so unnecessary. Gibson was trapped and helpless. There was no way he could avoid the blow. Even by the lore of the forwards that was a lousy foul for anyone to commit. Mike was out cold, and from then on he was virtually out of the game.

Another time du Preez raked me with his studs, but perhaps I deserved it. He stamped on my legs. I was at the bottom of the ruck: the law of jungle there. The referee penalized me. I openly disagreed. He looked at me, blew the whistle and stopped the game. I behaved all young and scared, my eyes like saucers. So he called up Tom Kiernan.

'This player just swore at me captain,' he barked.

I interrupted. 'No, I didn't. I was talking in Welsh.'

Tom then coasted in with his lovely Irish accent, 'To be sure that's true. To be sure it's only Welsh he's talking ref.'

The referee nodded and said, 'Oh! I see. Alright skipper I'll apologise to him.'

I accepted Mr Schoeman's apology like an angel. I ought to add that I've never told Tom what I really said.

Let me tell you what I think about the law of the jungle. Rugby is a physical game, and I have accepted my kicks and bumps as well as anyone else, but I have never agreed with foul play. I have been lucky too; I have never had a stitch put in a single cut. However, I have seen heads kicked and faces punched by thugs who pretend to be sportsmen. I have seen referees opt out of their responsibilities, and I have had to look down on injuries to players which have made my stomach turn. I have felt sick.

Only twice I have been afraid on the field. I have been afraid, once playing for Cardiff against Neath in 1967 and again facing Canterbury with the 1971 Lions.

In the Neath match the first sound I heard at the kick-off was a war cry, 'Charge', coming from their pack. Within minutes there was a viciousness about the game which frightened me. The boots were flying in, fights going on off the ball and I honestly thought someone was going to be killed. It was eighty minuites of mayhem, and fixtures between the clubs were cancelled.

Rugby should never be like that. I remember Bill Sam in my schooldays failing to answer a question on rugby for the first time. A young lad asked, 'How do you overcome fear, sir?' Bill just shook his head. He was right not to make up an answer. There is no reply.

As for the Lions in Canterbury, all hell broke loose at

the first line-out. The ball was thrown in and the whole Canterbury pack turned and started thumping us. Everyone knows how battered Sandy Carmichael was. His eyes closed up and you could hardly recognise him. Ray McLoughlin broke a thumb. With my own eyes I saw Fergus Slattery held down and a fist smash into his face, cracking out two teeth.

How do you combat this sort of play? Sadly the way which turned the Lions into winners not losers was 'to get the retaliation in first'. That became a necessity before triumph in 1974 in South Africa. To the call, 'Ninety-nine', the whole Lions pack waded in. Safety in numbers was the only way to quell the riot and get back to the skills again.

You may ask about the refereeing. That is where the trouble starts. I heard the referee of that Canterbury nightmare say to John Dawes, 'I've had enough. What happens now is up to you.' That was after only twenty minutes play.

I suppose rugby players accept injuries as part of the action. I have learned to ride punches and defend myself with my forearm, but I know that only the poor players are interested in dirty play. The best players want the ball, and the ball comes before the man in their sights.

For example, a week before the Canterbury game I had played against Otago and had come off the field with a cut lip, black eye and bruised ribs. But I was never fouled. It was an excellent game. I had simply been rucked by the whole pack. I came out like a spinning top, but that is the way it is in New Zealand. I accept that. That is the law of the field. It is the law of the back-street I am most angry about.

If anyone had seen the state of Ian Hall's leg when it was broken in a heavy tackle against New Zealand at Cardiff, they would never dream of inflicting injuries on another player by intention. It is crazy. That was a genuine accident, but the sight of his bones piercing his skin, and the leg snapped at right angles was enough to make me feel faint. Just think, a boot on the head could crack a skull. It is as easy as that. Luckily for me there was a sort of union agreement which prevented lock forwards from thumping scrum halves, and I am sure that if you told a couple of big forwards that punching is foul play they would be amazed to learn it.

In a Cardiff–Aberavon match once, Bill Mainwaring had a non-stop slogging affair with Ian Robinson. It was thump after thump. But then afterwards they were drinking together, Robbo greeting Bill with a slap on the back and, 'Hey Bill, that was a great punch you got me with in the second half. What you want – a pint?'

Referees have to be strict, especially at the start and must have enough understanding of the game to draw the delicate line between robust play and plain thuggery. Someone could get killed.

Back to South Africa and happier days.

It was on that trip that I made one of my greatest friends, another Irishman, Roger Young. We were competing for the scrum-half place, but that very situation brought us closer together. We were always to be seen together and would always wish each other well before a Test selection. Roger was modest and said that his chance would only come if I broke down. I did and he played in the third Test. Off the field we were inseparable.

There was a sequel. In the Irish match against Wales the following season I decided that my competitiveness would be affected if I treated Roger as a close friend. I gave him a few sharp nudges early on and when he called for the ball to put it into the scrum I scowled and growled, 'Get stuffed you Irish b —.' He looked at me really upset. I don't think he could believe it. Neither could I. But then as the game went on I began to think about what I had said to him.

Soon it was my turn to put the ball in. Roger picked it up and threw it to me saying, 'Where are we going tonight, then? Got the pretty Welsh girls lined up?'

That was too much for me. I broke down and

laughed. 'I don't know,' I said. 'What the hell can I do with you!' We were the only ones on that field who laughed that day. It was the game Wales won 24–11, in which Brian Price was lucky not to have been sent off for thumping Noel Murphy.

Ten years later I was able to reflect on South Africa and how she lies twisted in the political weeds. I am sad about it.

Our welcome in South Africa has always been the best, the most hospitable in the world. The people there, especially those who have British ancestry, have a special feel for us. Perhaps there are many Afrikaaners who are more abrupt, but that is often because they are not confident conversing in the English language.

I am sure that the overall affection is for our traditional way of playing rugby, the open running style which nearly always came second when the points were added up. When I went there first, all the talk was of Cliff Morgan, Tony O'Reilly, Butterfield and Davies and what was seen to be a glorious off-the-cuff approach.

In Britain, the Springboks have presented several faces. Often they have stuck to themselves – again the reluctance to converse in English has been the anti-social factor, and also, to be fair to them, our officials have tended to organize more after-match functions than we ever have to endure out there. I especially admired the Springboks of 1969–70. They stuck to their task despite the terrible background of demonstration and violence. They were herded together and the joy went out of the tour because of that, but everyone who played against them agreed that they kept the deep sporting feeling between the two countries alive and well.

It would be too easy to remember South African rugby as stereotyped, but that is a cheek, because we in Wales have almost reached the stereotyped style, in my opinion. I do recall big centres like Joggie Jansen, built like Delme Thomas, knocking over opponents but rarely looking to beat a man, but after my last trip out there in August 1977 I could see fresh thinking behind the scrum. Young men like Peter Kirsten and others showed off their natural athleticism behind the scrum.

South Africa is the one place in the world where running rugby should be played. The grounds are firm and dry. Whereas the mud of New Zealand and sometimes in Britain saps your strength and your zest, the ground in South Africa sorts out the athletes from the donkeys. The ball bounces about, and the ruck ball nearly always springs back cleanly. It suited my moving style. I even felt like training! As a country they breed athletic men. The boys in school look healthier and bigger than we do at the same age.

In retrospect, in 1968, we ran into some excellent players and our game was not particularly organized. The likes of du Preez, Myburgh, Ellis, Greyling, Bedford, Visagie and the rest needed no more encouragement than that.

Then in 1974 we were the organized party with a fine pack. We almost won too much ball. Frivolous passing, we thought, could lose us the initiative. We decided never to hand away the control, so we drove forward behind my kicks from scrum-half or Phil Bennett's. Of all the Springboks I respected and felt sorry for in 1974 it was Hannes Marais. He was one of the world's outstanding prop forwards and personally played very well against us. Yet I doubt whether he should have been brought back to captain the Tests. He should have been allowed to graze on the richest pastures of retirement. He never had a settled outfit; the press were fiercely critical of him just because he was on the losing side. The Lions got better and better while the great hero of many a Springbok victory grew visibly smaller. Only when the final Test was shared did Hannes receive any public credit. He deserved better because he was not only a great player, he was a gentleman. His defeats were bitter, but he was first into our dressing-room with a can of beer. He was not used to losing, but he knew how to do it with honour.

Of the other Springbok players I remember Dawe de Villiers the most vividly. Neat and competitive, he had all the attributes of a Test scrum-half. His running, kicking and passing were all skilful. Then Piet Greyling who in my mind went hand in hand with Jan Ellis; Greyling the destroyer, Ellis the scorer. Greyling was one of the best flankers I ever played against. He was hard and physical, and you always knew you had been in a contest against him, but again, he was a most friendly man off the field. Jan Ellis too was always happy to take us back to his house and show us his fine rugby collection over a few beers and a swim.

I am bound to leave out someone from this brief appreciation of South African friends and foes, but there is no way I could forget Choet Visser, who was liaison officer to the 1974 British Lions. He would have chosen fifteen Orange Free State players for every Test and certainly prayed that his men would beat the Lions. However he identified with our dreams of success too, spared no effort to look after our needs, and smiled when we won. Every single Lion will remember him with affection and admiration. He never panicked; always had the emergency under control. He personified all that was best in the rugby of the country.

It is impossible to have toured South Africa without having run up against the influence, if not the person, of Dr Danie Craven. When I first went out there in 1968 with Cardiff he was a legend. I remember asking him for his autograph. His conversation on rugby and on many other topics was thoughtful, intelligent and illuminating. It was possible to disagree with him, but there was never any doubt about what he was trying to say.

He simplified rugby and most of his criticisms were based on his realization that rugby is a simple game. He changed with time as you might expect. The iron fist of South African rugby dogma was unclenched slightly. In the end, if he was given a chance to speak after dinner he would embark on a history of British–South African relationships so deep and sensitive that he would take some stopping. But then he has a lot on which to look back; lots of friends, tries, penalty goals, games won and lost and now, so little to which he can look forward. Memories are getting thinner. We will not be able to live on them for ever.

8

Off my mind

In my playing time, rugby football has become big
business. Television coverage, with splendid colour pictures and knowledgeable commentary, has given the
game a wide entertainment appeal. Rugby has therefore
become commercially attractive to large manufacturing
firms who are looking not only for a television outlet but
also for a wholesome, traditional sporting image.

Live television coverage of international rugby has
done nothing to diminish the demand for tickets for
seats at the games, indeed appeal funds and debenture
schemes have been run to raise money to erect massive
grandstands all round the world from Loftus Versfeld to
Cardiff Arms Park.

The image of the players has changed. In an advertising world which grabs the conspicuous television 'personality', the most eye-catching rugby players receive
more and more approaches to appear on television and
become associated with companies. In the days when a
great player like Jack Kyle was playing for Ireland, no
one but the closest followers of the game would recognize him out of his own locality. In the seventies, when
Dave Duckham was a British Lion, he could not walk
down the main street in Cardiff without half a dozen
people coming up to him and talking to him. That can
be a nuisance for the player. Occasionally I found it
quite warming to meet someone who got pleasure from
my play. That is flattering. Others were bores who
never watched matches, but just watched TV chat

shows. Obviously, it is annoying too, because if I have to be recognized, I would rather it be for my rugby not my TV chatter.

Even the administrations of the rugby unions have had to change as the game has expanded. Long gone are the days when the secretary of the Welsh Rugby Union kept minutes in copperplate handwriting and stacked up the international tickets for 'domestic' sale on his kitchen table. Nowadays there has to be expertise in a more commercial world, backed up by legal and accounting ability.

Everything has been for the game's good as far as I am concerned, save one aspect. I do not believe that the Unions nor the general public appreciate how much the modern game has altered the demands upon the players themselves. There are committee men who pay lip service to current opinions, but you can still see them chanting on about *their* day. All they had to cope with was a few pints after the game and to remember the words of *Eskimo Nell*. At this particular moment in 1978, as I leave the field after eleven years of international rugby, I would ask for one change, and that is for a more generous attitude to the international player.

I do not mean that he should be paid, but I do believe a more realistic slice should be taken out of big-match expenses so that he can stay in the best hotels, eat and enjoy himself without too much restriction and involve his wife too. When you play in a match which has attracted a gate worth over £150000 you do not want to stay in a second- or third-rate hotel. Nor do you wish to be told that only one bottle of wine is allowed between four, that telephone calls to your home are to be paid by you and so on. For special duties, which have required years of effort (as well as of pleasure), you need special treatment when it can be afforded. Advertising and television income surely make it possible.

It is not so long ago that Scottish and Irish players were given one jersey only for an international season.

If they decided to swop with other countries then they had to buy the replacements. Even now that kit is sponsored, a Scotsman told me that their Union still makes them pay a nominal price for it. Maybe that sort of rule safeguards the citadel of amateurism.

Let me briefly discuss some of the pressures as Gareth Edwards has seen them. When I had a dozen or so caps to my name I was delighted by the public recognition and very rarely turned down invitations to speak at dinners. Even if it was on the other side of the country, say Newcastle, I would drive up there, speak, turn around and get back for work in the morning.

Suddenly I realized that many clubs (that is not to say Newcastle) did not truely appreciate my efforts. All they wanted was someone who was a 'draw' to sell all their tickets, and then to act like Bob Hope to give them an amusing end to their dinner. That was all right, but what was I getting out of it? My conscience told me that I was contributing to the game of rugby football, which had given me so much. Yes, I concede that, but I was losing a lot too. What about my wife and family? What about my employer who had to put up with me tired or late for work the next morning? These days, I am still delighted to give all I have got to the rugby fraternity, but I tell them my view straight away. I still say yes I am delighted to come, but they must fly me from Cardiff to Newcastle, with my wife if it is a mixed function, or see that we can get there comfortably by rail, and back to work in the morning. That is the change in values I mentioned. Instead of the vast and devouring public leaning on the player, they should make his visit to them practical in the context of work and family, and enjoyable.

Before there is a revolt among those who are famous for their hospitality, and that includes Newcastle I must emphasize, let me acknowledge the fun I have had with all those who have understood, and have added that touch of icing on the cake by recognizing the pressures.

The demands have escalated. Apart from the actual

rugby, which involves matches, travel, squad practices, sports forums, dinners, dances, raffles, auctions, opening shops and stores, there is the interference with your private life. There is no way that my wife and I can have a night in complete privacy in a restaurant near home. Television, or rather the result of it, has no mercy.

Relationships with one's club can be confused too. These days everyone has squad practice nights and it is considered a point of loyalty to attend. All the Cardiff boys will tell you that I have not been too keen on training, but at one stage there was a lot of criticism flying around, from players and Cardiff supporters, that I was not practising or playing enough. This was at the beginning of the 1977-8 season. I had just come back from a short tour of South Africa.

I remember getting my viewpoint off my chest. I said I believed that rugby was still an amateur sport, and that I liked to think, when I woke up in the morning, that I could have a game or go back to sleep. That exaggerates the situation, because I would not want to let down any side, but it emphasizes the amateur approach, that my life is mine and that it was my choice at the end of the day. Looking back now I can see that my attitude was a natural reaction to the life which had been very much imposed on me.

Let me recall a conversation I had in New Zealand. A rugby coach introduced me to a twenty-one-year-old boy and said, 'Look at this silly boy, Gareth; one of the best potentials in New Zealand. He is bound to be an All Black. But d'y'know what he has done Gareth? He has packed up the bloody game . . . yes, at twenty-one!'

The boy stood with us, but not all embarrassed by the comments. I asked him why he had chosen to do it. 'Because, for fifteen years I have been involved in competitive rugby and quite truthfully, I have had a gutsfull.'

How could you argue with that?

Also in an amateur game, the press, many of whom

have never played the game to international level, should think hard before they wade in with heavy criticisms. I have told in earlier chapters how the press worried me when I had those problems with my passing. They did not help me then and one of two were wrong in their judgement about me making the grade. The best and most acceptable writers are sympathetic. Vivian Jenkins was fair because he rarely criticized a player. If he mentioned your name in his match reports you had been good. Obviously there has to be a more constructive approach to mid-week writing about team-balance and general tactics, but that can be done in a cooler frame of mind with a day or two to think the problems through.

Just imagine how a player feels when he shuts himself away from all the family fun over Christmas and New Year, because he has four club matches and a Final Trial in that period. Or again the frustration when he has travelled up and down the M4 to London for the day, turns around and comes back knowing that the game did not go well. He grabs his bag of chips *en route* and gets home after midnight. On the next day he reads that reporter Joe Bloggs, the one man who is making some money out of the game, has written, 'What the hell was Cardiff's scrum-half doing there in the first place?'

It is history now that player concerns such as these came to a head in New Zealand on the Lions tour of 1977. It was natural that they should, because it was a losing campaign played in rain that rarely stopped for five months. The breakdown of good relationships with the press was sad. The media are not all evil. They have given people a much more intelligent understanding of rugby and what player is to say that the unbiased, off-the-field opinion is sometimes not the right one! On tour the press were always part of the team and the best characters among them never trespassed on players' territory.

I would not dream of expressing an opinion of my

own about events out in New Zealand '77, I was not there. However, I know that the Lions, all good friends of mine, came back disconsolate. They had one more assignment left, to play against the Barbarians at Twickenham in a game staged to raise money for the Queen's Jubilee. Although they had agreed to play the match before they had left for New Zealand, they suddenly shocked the rugby administrators by refusing to turn out. Basically the problem was that only fifteen Lions and replacements were invited to the celebrations. The Lions felt that the whole party should be there with their wives too or girl-friends. The cost out of a £200 000 gate would be negligible. They got their way in part, though they were booked into a modest hotel in Richmond. It was just another way of cutting costs at the players' expense. A couple of nights in Fawlty Towers! Some home-coming!

By the end of the game the dissatisfaction had grown. I am certain that the right attitude should have been, 'Right, let's give these boys, and their wives who have been without them for the whole summer, a great time: a reward for their efforts.'

No, we were all stuck in pokey little rooms, set-menu food, and wine only if your paid for it yourself. I asked the committee representatives if we could have some wine on my table because the Frenchmen Rives and Skrela were with me. There was a discussion and then the judgement. 'Yes, the French can have some wine, and because you are with them you can have some too.' This simple incident emphasized the embarrassment we always felt with the French, who always gave us a magic time at no cost to us in France. I looked at the wine list and was in a mind to choose the very best and most expensive they had, but I compromised and selected a wine of medium price which we all liked. Would you believe it? – ten minutes later the wine waiter returned with a bottle of ordinary plonk. Someone along the line had slipped him the committee motto, 'We can't waste money on the players.' The French boys saw the funny side of it. I wanted them to get up and walk out of the hotel in protest. I was furious. Then I cooled down because no one wants to start thinking that way.

The Lions told us about some of the restrictions they had suffered on tour, but we did have fun and settled for a good night at the Hilton on Saturday after the game.

Now it was the glossy West End and the dinner was superb. At last I managed to do the Frenchmen a favour. The waiter at our table had a chat with me about the game. I asked him to give us a bit of extra attention and slipped him a pound note. I was thoroughly enjoying a full, tasty trout when there was a tug on my cuff. Jean-Claude Skrela had finished his in lightning time and he wanted another. A nod and a wink to my waiter friend, and trout number two was in front of Jean-Claude.

The day was a success, the dinner superb, and all went happily until later in the evening. We had all withdrawn to a bar to enjoy our drinks. Then an announcement came that at that bar we had to pay for everything we wanted from now on; it was suddenly a pay-bar. Gerald Davies, the Babas captain, went to complain to Micky Steele-Bodger, one of the committee. Quickly a barrel of beer was organized for the players. 'But neither my wife or I drink beer,' protested Gerald. When asked what he would drink, he said lager would suit him, but not for his wife.

The reply came after a brief investigation. 'I have fixed you a free pint of lager, but no more, but there is nothing else available unless you all pay.'

As always, we ended up passing a pound note for every drink we ordered across the bar – that was about the going rate at the Hilton, and of course, we all looked after the Frenchmen. I do not think they would have believed us this time if we confessed that we were spending all our own money at an official function, after helping to fill Twickenham to capacity that afternoon.

I have never wanted to be paid for playing rugby. Like so many Welsh rugby players I have sat in my living-room with my mother and father at home and seen a rugby league representative take sheafs of pound notes out of his pocket and put them on the sideboard, but I have never failed to recognize my need to live among the people of South Wales. It is my part of the world, and that is the way I like it. I therefore want to be respected by my friends in the rugby world, and going north would have damaged my happiness, if not my bank balance.

Yet travel has opened my eyes. Getting Wales in perspective is important if you choose to live there. Similarly, weighing up British rugby against rugby overseas is equally illuminating. In so many respects the British game is delightful to play because there are teams for all talents and every attitude. I recall travelling down to Llanelli with the Welsh British Lion wing J. J. Williams. We passed through Hendy and saw forty or so rugby players going hard at it in their own local squad session. 'I could never do that at this level,' we said almost together. But then I smiled. They may never be international players but nothing in the world can stop them having their fun and their few pints. I think I have put a few too many balls in too many scrums to join in with the Cymgors extra Bs now, but whoever you are, and whatever your inclinations there is always a game for you in Britain.

However, I am writing this at a time when Kerry Packer is trying to create a brand of cricket, with super-Tests, closely linked with commerce and television. Often I have been asked if it would work in rugby. As long as the top rugby union players are paying their own hotel extras, and being denied a certain amount of privilege in a hugely sponsored game, then the ground is ripe for a Packer coup. No one is going to concede that it will work, but the presence of South Africa looms not too far away on the other side of the world, a magnificent rugby country, cut off from international competition, and they will always be ready to accept teams of international standing, and look after them superbly. I was privileged to be one of the scrum-halves in a world team which went out to celebrate the centenary of rugby in Pretoria. The moment we arrived, the Transvaal officials demonstrated their appreciation of our efforts to take part. We stayed in the best hotel in Pretoria; all expenses put down to our room numbers. No one was to be out of pocket whatever they did. In the three weeks we were allowed three telephone calls home. We were kitted out with a blazer, pair of slacks, a couple of pairs of shoes, even underpants; rugby boots, track suits, badges, cuff-links ... you name it, we had the very best. There was even a jersey for every match so that we could exchange one with an opponent if we wanted.

Chatting to Gerald Davies in our hotel room later, we agreed that everyone at home in rugby administration would think this extravagant. However we were certain that this is the way the British game should move to treat its players. It would be an incentive to get to international standards. In our first team meeting out there in Pretoria our manager, Syd Millar, and captain, Willie John McBride, got the same response from everyone before they could say anything, that we must be as good as our welcome. Rather quaint combination that, Millar and McBride, laying down the law in the country which they had set on fire, literally, with burning shirts back in 1968.

It was on this trip that I met my old pal, Roger Young. Roger was now a dental surgeon in Cape Town. I asked him to dinner at the hotel one night. We sat at the table, mulling over the old days, when one of the Western Province boys came to us and said, 'So glad you two have found each other. Do enjoy your reunion and your dinner. Drink what you like, have a good bottle, I've told the restaurant manager to put the whole bill on my account.' With a smile he turned and went. I can almost guarantee that it would not happen in Britain.

Then again, instead of the two match tickets free and two to buy which we are so used to, there were tickets for everyone who genuinely wanted to repay hosts by giving them seats for the game.

Apart from the personal comfort and treatment there are two more important considerations, the family and work. The family situation is never ideal and for some time the only words Owen, my first boy, could say were, 'Dada gone.' Maureen never once put pressure on me to give up, but I know now that she has taken enough absence for one lifetime. I have been lucky in her and also in my employer Mr Jack Hamer. I have never been deprived of my salary when I have been on tours. Other boys have.

On the first Lions tour I went on, the daily allowance was eleven bob a day. It went up to fourteen shillings and, of course, to a student £10 a week was a lot of money. Not that there was a need to spend much in those days, because we were well looked after. Now, however, our standards have risen so much *because* of the game, that certain things, as I have written, annoyed the 1977 Lions immensely.

They had a rise in daily allowance because of inflation to £3 a day, £21 for the week. When I was on tour I had no family commitments. I did not have to pay the gas bills. You see the Inland Revenue or the Electricity Board do not care if you are in New Zeland having your head kicked in for the sake of the flag. They still send you the bills.

The ultimate justice is for the rugby unions to pay your employer too when you have to go off to yet another squad practice or travel away. Or else do not have such long tours and so many training squads.

Beware! Professional rugby football could come, and will be of a higher standard than anything we part-timers can produce. The mood is ripe among players, as it was for Kerry Packer with the cricketers, for a privateer to step in. Towards the end of an international career, players less fortunate than me, who have no satisfactory job, would be easily persuaded to tour the world for the right reward for their families.

9
Home, work and play

Let me start with play. I always did, and I think both my wife Maureen, and my employer, Jack Hamer, would both faint if I suddenly lost my enthusiasm just because I have given up rugby football.

I have told you briefly how much fishing means to me; it is more than a sport. If I could fish every minute of every day, that would be part of heaven. I suppose it is in the blood from the early days. There is so much to learn – the worm, the spinner, the fly, and all the waters of the world, or at least my world, Wales.

I am not outstanding in the breed of true fishermen, but I am learning. I have taken out my 18½ lb salmon, and season by season I grow to know more about the habits of my prey under the water. Give me a rod and good water and I get carried away. Time comes and goes before I notice it; night and day are just visitors shifting on the surface of the water.

I am never too tired to go fishing. Even after a late night, I can still be off on the road to the river with my friends at four in the morning. Then, when you are driving along empty lanes, the countryside comes to life; the birds are out and the colours grow richer as the sun climbs up. Fishing is so much more than pulling a fish out of the water and putting it in a pot. It is to do with nature and the fun of your friends.

One of the presents I appreciated most of all was given by the Llandyssul Angling Association when I came home after the successful British Lions tour of

1971. They gave me five years fishing on the Teifi with their compliments to 'give back a little of the satisfaction you and the Lions gave us.'

Unfortunately, I have been so busy over the last two years, I have not been able to get down to the lovely river which swirls down from the Cambrian Mountains, through Lampeter, Llanybyther, Llandyssul, Newcastle Emlyn, and finally is channelled into the sea by the twin points of Cenmaes Head and Gwbert.

The Llandyssul boys taught me so much. Artie Jones and Jack 'Alma' (Alma's is simply the name of his shop) quickly made me see how little I knew. They loved teaching. Jack Alma was with me when I caught my big salmon. He was delighted, because he was a purist and I had done everything right. I am not sure how Artie received the news. I think like all good competitive fishermen he was saying to himself under his breath, 'I wish I had got that one myself.'

Graham Evans, a Swansea solicitor, is another of my angling friends, and what a superb companion. We laugh sometimes until we are weak at the knees. One night there were four of us fishing the River Tawe in pitch darkness, Graham, our mate Norman Jenkins called Jenks, Graham's brother John and me: no moon, not a chink of light. Although it is true that one's eyes get accustomed to the darkness, we were actually fishing 'blind', just by touch. I don't care how brave you are, it is a frightening experience. You never know what is around, you can just hear the scuffle of the badger in the bushes or the owl swishing through the air past your nose. We were spaced out along the bank and it was in this eery atmosphere that Graham and I heard old Jenk's reel scream out in the night. That was enough to shake me but I quickly wound in my own line to give him room to play the fish. Judging by the sound, he must have had a big one tearing away there. But, nothing happened, just silence along the bank. Then suddenly Jenks yells out 'Jasus, what in hell's. . . .'

Probably lost it I thought. A minute later another,

'Jasus, not again,' from Jenks hit the air. Again we both got out of the way to give him space. Silence. Nothing happened until there was a third scream 'Oh. B'Jasus Jones. . . .'

Time we looked into it. 'Hell, Jenks. What's going on down there?' We groped our way down.

He was furious. 'I threw my line out across the river and I thought I had a fish, but what happened was that a bat flew into it and grabbed on. Bit me on the bloody thumb. I threw the line back but the bat was hanging on. It bit me the second time, and then the third, the black b——.'

You can imagine how we laughed in the dark. We were like kids, and once we got the giggles we could not stop. Graham started it by saying, 'Hey Jenks. Look at that hair sprouting on the backs of your hands.' 'Hey Jenks, I don't remember your teeth sticking out like that before.'

It was one of the funniest fishing trips of my life.

Let me write again of one of my favourite characters from Gwaun-cae-Gurwen, the man we called Hywel Awful. An honest rogue and a fine fisherman who sometimes took short cuts in his art and 'borrowed' water too! When I was away in New Zealand in '71, the worst news I had from home was that Awful had been trapped by the bailiff for poaching. Not only that, but he had decided in the heat of the moment to let the bailiff feel the warmth of his right fist!

But what a character!

Poor Hywel had false teeth trouble. He could not wear his false teeth for more than a couple of minutes because he reckoned they always made him sick. If he was off to a party or dance he would carry his teeth in his pocket until he considered it essential to transfer them to his mouth. On Friday nights, before going out fishing, Awful and I used to have a bag of fish and chips and eat them in the kitchen. Then, on the table he would mix his 'jams', his poaching pastes. I would say, 'Now look here Awful I don't want to be involved. Just imagine the *Western Mail* telling everyone, "Welsh scrum-half caught poaching".'

But Awful would be deep in concentration by now, loving his task of mixing the salmon eggs into a flour paste: deadly for trout. Those tactics would kill the sport for me, but it was not that Awful wanted to catch a hundred fish at once, simply that he loved the risk. It was in his nature. This was the ritual to be played out before every trip: the mixing of the paste, the secret recipe, the anticipation. I never lived by Awful's law. . . . Scout's honour.

And there was another Awful speciality. He never had any tackle. On the other hand, I always had too much like every normal fisherman; five rods, boxes of this and boxes of that. Awful was always, 'lend me this and lend me that'. I have seen smart fishermen well dressed with the best rods, furious when they see Awful catching every fish in the river (legitimately this time), with a broken-down old rod which he just slings into the coal shed at home when he finishes, along with his wellies which I believe fell off some lorry or other. Hywel went down West to live. We went separate ways.

Back to fishing. Another fishing friend of mine was Clive Gammon, a very cultured, witty man, who had such a wide knowledge of the sport. He was a professional angling correspondent, and it was he who talked me into joining him in an International Fishing Race for television. We went over to Sweden as one team, with two others representing Britain. It meant ten days in Sweden with really hard competition for what they called the world's smallest prize, the Golden Maggot. I had never done any coarse fishing and very little sea fishing, so I knew that I was unlikely to win, but it looked like fun. The winners were to be decided by the quantity of their catch at three venues.

We arrived by boat in Gothenburg. The caravanettes which were to house us were tucked up in the hold and inside them were the secrets, we hoped, to British success, maggots.

I do not mind the sight of a golden maggot, but the real thing squirming in those buckets turned my stomach. However, the coarse fishermen played with them as if they were toying with their own lives, gently, affectionately, making sure that they were not moist or sweaty, feeding them and . . . ugh! Enough.

Imagine my reaction in the morning when Clive and I went down to the hold of our caravanette. There were maggots in the fridge, in the cooker, in our clothes, everywhere.

I immediately panicked and thought that we had been sabotaged by the two other teams. We cleaned them up as well as we could, but there was no way we could get them all out of the mat, or the corners. From then on Clive and I kept our tackle in the caravanette but slept in hotels. However, our friends Kevin Linane and Terry Eustace, and the defending champions, Gibbonson and Gillespie slept among their buckets of maggots each night. Honestly, I would not have thrown chickens in there.

First we went to the south of Sweden while the second team went right across Sweden to Stockholm, and the third up to Lapland.

It turned out to be the most exhausting few days of my life. We drove about three or four hundred miles to our first destination and went to bed at ten o'clock. We started fishing at daybreak and fished eighteen hours until nine in the evening. I was almost too tired to go to bed. Next morning we were up at six and set off on the journey from the south, seven hundred miles to Stockholm. I was too tired to have dinner when we got there. I just slept, and was up again at two o'clock in the morning for another eighteen hours at the water's edge. It was the same the next day, flying north to Lapland in a little single-engined plane which shook the guts out of me and brought back memories, especially as I was still having nightmares about those horrible twisting maggots.

However, I must admit, there followed the most

memorable of all my fishing experiences.

We stayed in log cabins and the most hospitable Lapps looked after us. At meal times they demonstrated their skill and custom of transforming the most ordinary fish, which we would probably only give to the cat, into a meal for millionaires. Beautiful . . . and all this in front of a blazing log fire.

When I landed I almost wanted to die; now after such a warm welcome and with a sight of the most beautiful lakes, I could not wait to get out my rod and that is exactly what I did, even though it did not count in the competition.

The water was so clear. I could see down fifteen feet quite easily to the huge boulders, which they say had come down, plunging into the waters, from glaciers. The fish we were chasing were grayling, a sort of poor man's trout, but they were big, about two, three and four pounds, and were tremendous fighters. The deep and fast-flowing waters added to the fight. We released the fish when we caught them and both of us agreed that this would have been a marvellous salmon river. Man had interfered, however, with that possibility, because about sixty miles down river there was a hydro-electric dam. Yes, if that had been a salmon river I would have saved up all the money I had to go out there every year, to the pure, clear air, the kind Lapps and of course the reindeer.

On the fourth day the scene had changed. It was three o'clock in the morning and we were fishing the river in front of the Royal Palace in Stockholm. Our warm breath steamed up into the freezing air through our beards. We had given up shaving. No fish were biting. The beauty of the lakes was behind us, and we were enduring the hardest part of the exercise, trying to land fish who were not prepared to play.

The television camera whirred from time to time, Ian Wooldridge of the *Daily Mail*, a working witness, huddled thoughtfully behind. At about five o'clock we were surprised to hear other living persons moving slowly but noisily down the road. Two young men were hanging on to each other. They had obviously had a good night out. They were whispering loudly and pointing at us. I was tucked away behind my collar. It was only their voices getting more argumentative on such a still night that made me turn round. 'There you are. Told you it was 'im. You *are* Gareth Edwards aren't you. Where's the game then? Sign this for us Gar.' They were unmistakably Welsh voices. It turned out that one of them was a singer working in a club in Stockholm. His brother had come out from their home in Barry to spend a holiday, and they were having a rare old time. Ian Wooldridge refused to believe it for some time. 'No, not in Stockholm,' he kept saying.

As the day got moving in Stockholm our whole environment changed. Fishing has always meant tranquillity and silence to me, the Teifi or the Wye Valley, the feeling of being part of nature – but Stockholm was suddenly different. Whereas it was perfectly calm outside the Royal Palace early in the morning, later, we moved on to the next venue in the Race, and I laughed to compare the fishing spots in Wales with this.

We were in the main street. . . .

It was strange to be sitting there in this street in Stockholm, a long fishing rod in my hand, casting the line over the railings into the river which was about fifteen feet below, while trams and buses were whizzing around behind me. It was like fishing in Oxford Street. Passers-by looked disapprovingly at this scruffy, bearded fellow with the bucket of maggots by his side. I looked like a tramp in search of a bite to eat. At least the fish were biting this time. Just show them a maggot and whoosh, they were on the end of the line, but I am glad no one spotted me there.

I suppose that recognition is a pleasure as well as a pain. In the autumn of 1977 I was out in Barbados with my family and friends, really relaxed, having a drink, when a chap comes up and says, 'You're Gareth Edwards aren't you? Do you want a game on Thursday?'

I had intended to train every day in my gym shoes, and so I said I would probably turn out. As it happened I played against these local boys, at their request, for a side raised by a frigate which had just docked in Bridgetown. The pitch was tough grass on the middle of the race course. I looked after myself carefully and we had some fun. I think my pals Nigel and Stephen Hamer only pushed me into playing because they fancied some drinks on the boat afterwards. We were not let down. It was so long since I had sat down in a sing-song after the game, banging out songs like *Dinah, Dinah*, as we used to many years ago. The game is there to be enjoyed. These boys enjoyed their game as much as I had enjoyed any game I had played in. Some of those West Indian lads are just ripe for some coaching too.

Alongside the public Edwards was the private young man who had to sort out a career. Although I was trained to teach, I fancied it less and less. I watched Barry John and Gerald Davies, who were teachers at the time, and saw that they were far from content with the life. What is more, as a physical education teacher I would have had to spend a lot of time in a track suit, and anyone who knows my training habits, or rather, my habit of non-training, will tell you that I was not made for that.

It was never a question of money. My first job was for a public company who were in the quarrying business. I was a trainee manager setting out to be a sales executive. I was promising.

My mind was confused at this time by offers to play rugby league. Several times I rejected offers of £15 000, but eventually sought the advice of Mr Hamer, father of Nigel and Stephen, the boys I had known at Millfield School. Jack Hamer's solution was an open offer, 'Work for me in Dynevor Engineering, if you want a settled mind. You many not be a millionaire, but your future will be safe.'

Whatever happens in the future I have enjoyed the

association, and confess that I could never have contributed so much to rugby football had it not been for the Hamer family.

I was out of college in 1969, and in 1972 I married that pretty, dark-haired girl from home, Maureen. She too has been marvellous about my going off to play rugby around the world. At the time of writing my family is four, Owen and Rhys are our boys.

Owen was born on a Tuesday in 1974, and on the Friday I joined the Lions to set out for South Africa. My next sight of Owen was in a photograph. Jack Hamer travelled out to see the first two Tests bringing with him photographs of the family. I took Owen's photo on the bus for the first Test. It lifted me. I'll never forget the feeling to the day I die. 'We'll win this one for you, *bach*,' I can hear myself whispering. It was like dedicating the bull to the President, or rather to someone you loved. 'This is going to be yours,' I repeated.

It was more a party than a bus trip back to the hotel, the Springboks had been 'done'.

I could have gone with the Lions next time in 1977 to New Zealand as far as Maureen and the Hamers were concerned. They were 100 per cent behind me, whatever I decided. In the end I said no, but it was not an overnight decision. I assessed the personal pleasures of spending a summer with my family, of continuing my advance at work, because I was by now shouldering more responsibility in senior management. Jack Hamer simply said 'If your family can manage without you for three months then I can.'

Maureen said simply, 'If you want to go, go. I know it will be important for you.'

The final decision was my own. I suppose there is nothing worse than knowing the enormity of the task ahead of you. New Zealand, especially after the Lions successes of '71 and '74, was going to be incredibly hard. What had I to prove? What would be the stimulus if I went? Did I even want to play for Wales again? I did not know the answer to any of these questions, and I realize now that I was, at that particular time, mentally played out.

The summer's rest had the effect of rejuvenation. I slowly began to feel less a slave to the game and more a true amateur. I could not even help out when requested as a Lions replacement half-way through the tour when Brynmor Williams and Doug Morgan struggled with injuries. I was unfit at that mid-summer stage, and the cure was only just having its effect. Yet when October came I was alert and eager to get my hands on a ball again, and once committed in the mind, dragged my body back . . . one more time.

My family in Gwaun-cae-Gurwen continued to be enthusiastic but not truly knowledgeable about rugby football. I think they watched number nine around the field quite a bit! Yet, I would have missed my father if he had not called into the Welsh dressing-room after a game. He never ever embarrassed me or pressured me; he just came and said, 'All right?'

I would say, 'Yes, fine Dad. Cup of tea?' He had a quick cuppa, chatted to one or two of the lads maybe and was off with my kit. He never stayed for more than five minutes, and I know he only came to make sure for my mother that I had not had a bump.

As for Bill Sam, he still kept in touch, but less so, of course. He picked up the telephone occasionally and announced, 'I hear you are not playing well.'

Yes, on the whole, he was a bit more complimentary by the end!

10

The rough with the smooth

In many ways I never liked the word 'coaching', I preferred to think of 'organizing'. That was what happened to Welsh rugby. Critics of early coaching theories moaned about the loss of flair. The performance of the Welsh team soon showed how individual talents could be given even more scope than ever before. Our thinking was ahead of other countries for a short time. Soon everyone was sharing the intricacies of turning the scrummage when the ball was lost, decoy moves bringing the full back into the game, and so many other touches which resulted from a clearer basic analysis and philosophy.

I have mentioned before that I was never first on to the training ground, but nearly always first into the showers. However, even I could see how important squad training sessions were. Preparation and planning were the bywords of Welsh rugby before the great seasons from 1969, the Triple Crown, 1970, the shared Championship with France and the 1972 the Grand Slam.

The '69 campaign opened with the bogey, Scotland at Edinburgh. We always went there with a lot of apprehension. I remember reading in the programme before the game that Wales had made eighteen visits to Murrayfield since it was opened in 1925 and had won only seven times. Scotland had won eleven. Then, since the war, Wales had won only four of eleven matches. Another thing made us uncertain; this was our first game, but Scotland had played against Australia in November and against France in Paris, an incredible match which Scotland won 6–3. We had two new caps, both youngsters, Williams, the London Welsh full back and Davies their back row forward! I was most interested in this Davies fellow. I could take a lot of stick from the Scots if he did not know his trade, and the only fact that stuck in my mind was that just three months ago he had been playing for some unknowns, the Old Guildfordians!

As it turned out, Merv the Swerve Davies knew his stuff and we won the game 17–3 simply by being better organized. In all the games which had gone before, international rugby had been a question of fervour against fervour with the home team raising its game that little bit higher. Now we were able to ride the ground disadvantage by method. Keith Jarrett was a key performer. Although we played into the wind in the first half, he kicked two penalty goals within ten minutes.

The Irish game in Cardiff was wild! The build-up in practice during the week had been urgent too. Ireland had beaten England and France in Dublin as well as Scotland at Murrayfield. This visit to Cardiff was to be only their second Grand Slam in Irish history. It was a hot sunny day, the Cardiff Arms Park was in some disarray because the new north stand was still under construction, but we ran out of a corner gate on to the field proudly before the Prince of Wales.

The echo of the anthems had scarcely died, when our captain Brian Price was swinging a haymaker of a punch into the face of Noel Murphy. What a dish to set before the . . . 29000 spectators saw it; it was no quiet affair. Murphy fell to the ground, clutching his face and it looked as if Ben Price was going to be sent off by referee Doug McMahan. He got a warning instead, and a penalty was awarded to Ireland. Murphy remained on the floor in a wriggling heap while all this went on. My Lions captain Tom Kiernan was leading Ireland,

and he raced up on to the scene from full back. 'You dirty beggars. This is the Murphy plan. I know. You can't kid me.' Some of the Irish team were doing a war dance; others like O'Callaghan, the prop, were giving us the cold killer-look. I thought that this was the end of the road as far as the game was concerned. Kiernan kept on muttering. 'Yes, 'tis the Murphy plan, the dirty. . . .'

Wales had definitely worked out a plan for Murphy, a player whom we thought to be dangerous on the flank of the scrum, but it was not to punch him in broad daylight, or even to foul him at all.

Our plan in training was to nullify his value to Ireland as a good talker, good player and a good pack leader. We wanted to make sure that he knew he was in a game all right, and so the plan was that I would pick up the ball from early scrums and run straight at him. He would obviously relish tackling me and then whoosh, the whole Welsh pack reckoned to be an inch behind to drive over him until he went a bit quieter and lost his appetite for tackling! We would not have practised it so much if it had just been a question of giving him a bang on the nose in the first five minutes. In our practice sessions the man who stood in for Noel Murphy was John Hickey. Poor fella got trodden into the ground by the end and he almost deserved a cap just for that performance. 'Don't ever ask me to be Murphy again,' he said as he showered.

This was a compliment to Murphy but how did Kiernan know that we had a Murphy plan? It happened in the style of MI5. An anonymous phone-caller contacted Tommy at his hotel, the Seabank, at Porthcawl. 'I am a friend of the Irish team. Watch out for the Murphy Plan.'

Tom to this day has never believed that Brian Price's punch was not the secret weapon. The truth was that I had not put the ball into the scrum up to the moment when it happened, so we could not launch our plan. Brian Price was acting in strict retaliation to a painful foul inflicted by Murphy himself in a maul.

I was young and frightened that the captain might be sent off. Murphy was groaning around, making a meal of it. Meanwhile the forwards had declared war. Could we stick to plans; to think and not to scrap?

In a matter of seconds there was a scrum. I waited to put the ball in. The forwards linked arms and lay back. In the red corner . . . in the green! Syd Millar, Ken Kennedy, another chatterbox, and Phil O'Callaghan were snorting almost fifteen yards away ready to drive in with a crunch. The Welsh front row by comparison had amiable-looking faces. Denzil Williams was always the most innocent-looking of all; Jeff Young had a permanent grin, and John Lloyd simply concentrated, tongue hanging out, as if the whole business was slightly academic. They hammered in for that scrum, bone crashed bone, there was a shout, and before the ball got in at all someone had hit the ground. It was an Irish shirt crumpled up in a heap. Kennedy was down. What now? The referee broke up the scrum to hear Denzil Williams, the old campaigner. 'Serves you right,' Denzil was nodding at an Irish second row forward. 'Got one of your own men. Serve them right,' he said, muttering as he turned away. It was brilliant acting. I am not sure who did it . . . well, perhaps I am, but all I shall say is that it was a virtuoso performance of its kind!

So again the Irishmen ranted. Anyone would have. Tommy Kiernan almost frothed at the mouth. He was threatening to take his players off the field. He turned to me as a touring mate. 'C'mon Gareth, get them to stop it.' I said that I had not seen it. 'Oh shut up,' he almost yelled. 'You're too young anyway.'

The game could have gone into a shambles, but luckily Wales began to play a bit well and it became more open. The patterns of Welsh success emerged. There was a certain amount of Irish revenge flying around. Brian Thomas had to go off to have stitches in one of the worst head wounds I have ever seen on the rugby field. In a way, that worked more against Ireland than

Wales. Brian returned after medical attention, rumbling like a rhinoceros to a scrum near the Taff end of the pitch. The scrum jolted forward about five yards with his personal effort – he was a magnificent scrummager – and the crowd went ooh! We were then only 8–6 ahead. We won that scrum, rocking the Irish back row. Barry John missed out both centres but found Stuart Watkins free on the right and he completed a superb sequence with a try. We won 24–11.

After the match, relations between the teams were a bit sour. It did not stop Roger Young and me enjoying ourselves. However, small wounds heal. If you could have seen me some years later in Cork where I had gone out to help Tommy Kiernan in a celebration match, you would have thought that Tommy and I had played on the same side all our lives. He gave Maureen and me the time of our lives. That's rugby.

France was the upset that year. We had a settled side but France made eight changes. I had what I considered to be my best game for Wales so far. I remember Keith Jarrett setting off on a run down the right flank and passing out to John Taylor. I pushed myself to get up inside John, and by the time he slipped the ball to me I felt my momentum was right to take on the French defence. They laid hands on me, but I went on. It was not running for running's sake. Remember I have made the point previously of body awareness which gymnastics taught me. I was half-stopped but I was able to turn and spin out of tackles. Within a few yards of the line there were quite a few Frenchmen restraining me in some way or another, but still my body knew that it had the balance and the drive to make another yard (that is if I was not throttled by my jersey!). Over I went.

In terms of planning however, I still get satisfaction from the try I set up for Maurice Richards. It was a delicate chip-kick to the left wing which got Maurice stretching, and away he went. What a marvellous sight he was in full flight.

Villepreux was the French hero. How everyone

underestimates the French courage! Ideas that they fall apart when they are down are pure history. It may have been that way in the fifties, but I can never recall anything but determination and trouble with them. This was 1969, and we had not won in France since 1957. They have always been extremely physical. I believe they need firm refereeing. They are raised by their own crowd as much as we are, and certainly criticized by their fans much more than any other country I know.

Villepreux put over a forty-five-yard penalty in the second half and then put a high kick into space. It bounced around awkwardly, and Campaes was in for a try which Villepreux converted. All I can remember from then on was the terrific noise from the crowd and Phil Bennett coming on for Gerald Davies. Poor Gerald dislocated his elbow; Phil never touched the ball at all in his first appearance on the international field.

We took England apart at Cardiff, 30 points to 9. We crossed their line five times, while all they got were three penalty goals by Bob Hiller. Again these facts are all recorded in the appropriate history books. My personal contribution was something that made me particularly proud. I was captain because Brian Price was injured, and although the Triple Crown was at stake and I wanted to win the prize all by myself, I concentrated on feeding Barry as well as I could. My reward and the reward for every Welshman was to see Maurice Richards score four brilliant tries. Welsh rugby had returned to old dimensions. Wingers were for scoring tries. Overlaps would release them as much as the midfield break. The fourth try was a touch of solo virtuosity, Maurice slicing in off that sharp side-step, never losing his speed, and baring his teeth, or rather the gap in his teeth, which always turned this most quiet man off the field into a tiger on it. Maurice was not to play another home international season for Wales. Two Tests against New Zealand lay ahead of us and one at home against South Africa before Christmas. He played those, but then, one day he wrote a letter to Salford rugby club *asking* if he could play rugby league.

At Salford then was David Watkins, my old partner. He told me later how amazed they were to receive that letter. Maurice was a player they would have paid for handsomely, but thought there was no chance of his leaving the union game in his prime. David was telephoned one day by his chairman, who told him about the letter and asked him to come and meet this player who 'says he is a Welsh international and British Lion'. The chairman had even forgotten his name. David could not even guess who it might be. Down at the Salford ground David's mouth dropped open to see Maurice there. Salford snapped him up for far less money than Maurice could have commanded if he had leaked the news northwards that he was 'interested'. Yet he was that sort of guy, so straight and honest; religious too. For a long time he sent the earnings from playing Sunday rugby to his chapel back in the Rhondda.

He was a loss to Wales. In the next season we were forced to play centre-three-quarters on the left wing. Ian Hall played twice, good and solid but not fast enough, Keith Hughes and Jim Shanklin.

So, with the Triple Crown perched on our heads, we set off with confidence for New Zealand that summer. Unfortunately we were embarking on one of the craziest itineraries ever devised and the Welsh Rugby Union must bear the blame for accepting it. Confused by jet lag, we held on to a 9–9 draw against Taranaki after only three days in New Plymouth. Then just three more days later we faced the full blast of the All Blacks at Christchurch. More important than excuses, these New Zealanders were the best side I had ever played against. Great names and rightly so – Meads, Lochore, Kirkpatrick, Going and that most effective full back, McCormick.

Our pack was pushed aside in two Tests, whereas our backs looked as if they might pull off surprises at any moment. It is certainly possible to criticize the big

Welsh forwards from whom we expected and needed so much, but ultimately we had to acknowledge, after beatings of 19–0 and 33–12, that we were nothing like good enough.

Deep conversations with coach Clive Rowlands on the way home threw up enough hope for the future. The younger players had done well and in fact were very inexperienced. They were babies, those boys like Keith Jarrett, J. P. R. Williams, Mervyn Davies, John Taylor, Maurice Richards, and so was I still at twenty-one. There was a fair chance that we would learn our lessons from New Zealand. Clive Rowlands definitely would understand that future trips would have to be more considerately planned, and that the interpretations of referees would have to be understood before we tackled the main games.

Another tribute to New Zealand in 1969 – they treated us like heroes even though we were made to look a clear second best. In a way it made me more determined to return to show that we could play better, given a stronger platform up front. When we moved on to Australia, winning at the Sydney Oval in a mud-bath by 19–16 at least there was a move of great significance which was to benefit Welsh rugby from then on. Gerald Davies switched to the wing from centre. I think Clive Rowlands was the man chiefly responsible. He saw Gerald's beautiful side-step smothered time and again in the centre, and once establishing that he was not short of speed, Gerald was happy to give it a go. In so many ways the New Zealanders had taught us the lessons which were to lead to their own undoing in 1971, but then rugby knowledge is not anyone's private property. On Lions tours, the four home countries contribute and share. Yet, as Wales in '69 travelled back through Fiji and were fêted by those most generous people, King Batu and all, I could not imagine that British forward play could ever come up to All Black standards. Their speed on the ball, the directness and the second phase momentum. The sheer repetition

Home thoughts from abroad. We'll win this one just for you,
Owen bach.

At home with Owen on the left, and Rhys.

Gareth and Gethin always on the move. Putting on a show for the neighbours in Colbren Square.

I cannot resist a single sport.
Kruger Park, South Africa.

Visiting a client, with my
employer, Jack Hamer (left).

On the management force at Dynevor Engineering Company,
Neath.

More than a sport, a passion. Dawn breaks on the Towy.

No one more competitive than J. P. R. Williams even during time off in Tokyo.

Gordon Broon of Troon 'nursing' his injured hand. Well, to be fair we found ourselves in rather distinguished golfing company. Gary Player points the way with a three wood.

The brilliant Andy
Irvine.

Another great flanker; power and
talent too in the massive shape of
Ian Kirkpatrick.

One more time. My last try for Wales, the twentieth, against
Scotland at Cardiff, 1978.

Out of harm's way this time. Kirkpatrick, Going and Wylie see the
ball move to the Cardiff backs, 1974.

Taking the fight to the old enemy.

The final seal. Buckingham Palace with Maureen and my dad.

made tackling almost a worthless sacrifice. It was, without doubt, a black summer for Wales.

By the following January, 1970, Wales were in a strange state of rebuilding, and as so often happened on these occasions they gave me the captaincy. I use the word 'strange' because the selectors fiddled with men out of position as they so often did against tourists, and it was time to face the South Africans. We took the field with J. P. R. Williams, Phil Bennett on the wing, Dawes, Raybould, Hall on the left; Barry John and me; Denzil Williams, Perrins, Barrie Llewelyn, Delme Thomas and Geoff Evans, Dai Morris, Mervyn Davies and Dennis Hughes.

The personal fascination about that match was that I did not believe I was anything like fit enough to play. I was definitely going to cry off. I had pulled a hamstring in a match a fortnight before and had been dashing along to Gerry Lewis, our physio, three times a day. Gerry nursed me through and got me to work gently within the limits of the injury. It took patience and of course, in your mind, you always imagine the situation where you have twenty yards to get to the line with the cover closing, just to score the winning try. It was almost like that.

Gerry Lewis did get me on to the field, but I truly felt that I would be off within half an hour. It was a day of appalling cold rain and mud. I could hardly tell who was who. I do not know how the spectators managed. We slugged it out like two big mountain fighters over endless rounds. South Africa had the edge. We had lost all six times in the past, slowly but certainly we were being sucked under again. They led with a penalty goal after twenty minutes but I levelled with a penalty goal from a wide angle. It is hard to believe now that Barry was not kicking goals for Wales in those days, but with Keith Jarrett gone North, we had to improvise.

Then, a short time into the second half, Syd Nomis got a fine try. I felt that the Springboks were tactically in charge. Somehow we had to break up the pattern;

but how could we do it in mud and rain?

Many will recall how the referee was virtually poised to blow the final whistle when our new winger Phil Bennett threw a long pass infield from the touch line. Barry punted the ball across field, in ran Ian Hall to rush the defensive efforts of Nomis, and from a quickly-formed ruck Barrie Llewelyn flipped the ball back to me. My first thought was my hamstring. Gently, gently I kept saying to myself, 'God there is not time for that, let it go.' Off I set, and felt nothing, on I went and saw only the line. The corner flag loomed up as a target at the feet of the ring of policeman who had mustered to control the anti-apartheid demonstrations. I dived, slithered and I was there. Dawe de Villiers, the Springbok captain looked as dead as I was alive now. The conversion was missed. The whistle sounded. Quietly I made my way to the dressing-room and looked for one man, Gerry Lewis.

Wales expects her warriors to do well wherever they are, whatever the circumstances. That is pressure, but it is also the price you pay for playing sport at the top. Just before I retired there was a lot of bleating among players about press criticism. Yes, as I have said elsewhere in the book, the writers ought to be reminded now and again that players are amateurs. However, I do not believe in shirking the job of being a public figure either. After a poor game my life is interrupted almost by the minute when I walk down the street. 'You struggled a bit there Gareth,' they will say. 'Hey, that Going bloke gave you an 'ammering, didn't he?' At the start I used to try and justify my performance a little, or point to the wet ball, or the lack of cover for me, or just say that I wasn't feeling too good. But I learned in the end to agree with them. They do not mean too much harm, and quite honestly it is the quickest way to end the conversation. Yet there was a time when it hurt. I knew they were right. I had not played well. Worse still I had gone off the field injured, and my replacement had a blinder!

That was in 1970. Wales had beaten Scotland at Cardiff 18–9. I was captain then against England at Twickenham. England played well enough to stop us getting any sort of rhythm going. There were twenty minutes to go; we were 6–13 down when I went in to tackle Nigel Starmer-Smith. As I caught hold of him and fell, Dennis Hughes our flanker, dropped right on top of my ankle. I twisted it badly and limped off. What was I to do? I sat at the side of the pitch for a while. I reckoned that I could go back on. Certainly in the days before replacements I would have done that. But now, thousands of Englishmen were raising the roofs off the stands because Wales were about to fall. The roars went through my brain in huge waves. I had to think straight and decide quickly.

Ray Hopkins was standing by, fit. He must go on, and so he did. Chico played brilliantly to turn defeat into victory in that space of time. The score was 9–13 when he pounced on a loose ball at the back of the line-out and weaved his way over for a try. J.P.R. got the all-important conversion, and finally Barry John dropped a goal. We were on course for the Triple Crown all right, but I was worried. If Chico Hopkins could play as well as that in twenty minutes, how much more could he do in a whole game? He was just the sort of player who would prove his worth in points. He virtually ran the Maesteg team from the scrum-half position. He had been given a chance and had taken it. The critics gave me a 'going over'. A lot said that Hopkins should play. So, I was relieved to be picked for the Irish match and still captain too. But greater disaster followed. That bleak day in Dublin was the day when Barry John and I grew up.

We had always been on the crest of a wave, Gareth and Barry, Barry and Gareth, one or the other would score; we always got through with credit. This time it was a double disaster. Not only did Wales fail to take the Triple Crown, but we were both poor. It was the worst game we had ever played together, and I cannot recall one after that which was so fatal to Wales. Full marks to the Irish. They disrupted us. Our possession was very ragged, and possibly because we were relatively inexperienced we found it difficult to react in a sensible way. The Irish in 1978 came at Wales in the same way when the Triple Crown was there to be won. Then I drew on every lesson learned back in '70 and kept a reasonable calm about me. In '78 I could think, in spite of the tornedo of Irish wolfhounds in green jerseys and the roar of their crowd. In '70 it was like an eighty-minute nightmare from which I could not wake up. The chief haunter was Ken Goodall. That is the best performance I ever saw from an Irish number eight forward. We lost without ever looking like winning.

Back at home Barry and I took some stick in the press, and all those tongues wagged again, especially in Maesteg of course, where Ray Hopkins lay waiting after an international career of twenty minutes of brilliance. The accolades were gone, the hangers-on disappeared. I found out quickly who my true friends were.

It may only be a game, but such a public upset teaches you a few of the harder facts of life. On the following Monday Barry and I decided to play for Cardiff down at Penarth instead of resting after the big game. It was the best way to ride the criticism which in my case was harsh because I had been captain too. 'He's too young to carry the responsibility,' I could hear them say . . . well, I could almost hear them say. That is another thing about experience – later on, you do not waste time worrying about what people are *not* saying. However, at that particular moment in 1970 I could hear the criticisms, read them in the papers, and I also imagined the world was against me.

From the touchline at Penarth, on a dismal damp evening with few watching, the voices in the crowd came through more clearly than usual. I threw an early ball to Barry – it was a lousy pass and he slipped and fell over. I then tried a sixty-yard dropped goal which went nowhere and the crescendo built up, 'Rubbish. You are worse than you were on Saturday.' We looked at each other and shrugged. 'That's what it's all about pal,' our eyes said.

Within days all sorts of rumours were flying about. It was vividly spread around that J. P. R. Williams and I had been fighting in the Welsh dressing-room after the match because J.P.R. had been 'knocking off Gareth's girl friend'. Yes that's the level the hero had reached, Welsh captain and all that, within days! I have said before that the greedy Welsh rugby public can devour you.

There was an incident with J.P.R., but it was on the field. There was a penalty kick given to Wales and I said, 'J.P.R., do you want to take this kick?' That was as good as saying, 'have a go' as far as I was concerned.

He replied with, 'You are the captain, you make the decision.'

So, I took that as meaning that he didn't particularly fancy it, so I said, 'All right, if that's your attitude I'll take it.'

I placed the ball just to the left of the posts, twenty-five to thirty yards out and looked up. Duw, I'd never seen narrower posts in my life. I kicked . . . and missed.

I can laugh at the ironies now. First of all, there was J.P.R. and I arguing as to who should take the kick when we had one of the great kickers in Barry John whistling in the background. He had not taken up kicking regularly at this time. Also, it should have been a moment of happiness for the Welsh half-backs, because that day we set a record of sixteen appearances together, beating the famous 'Dancing Dicks', Swansea's Dick Jones and Dicky Owen who played for Wales between 1901 and 1910.

However, something much more important happened. We were both fired in the heat of criticism. We became harder, tougher competitiors. That is the way with top sport. When the flames are around you, you either melt or emerge unbreakable, in spirit at least.

I kept my place in the Welsh team, but lost the captaincy. The onus had affected my play, it was thought. To date I had led Wales seven times and had achieved four victories as well as a draw against the Springboks. The team had been chopped and changed. I really had no chance to build up a winning era. I never had a winning team under me, but that season had shown signs of progress. John Dawes took over for the French match at Cardiff. He was unquestionably an excellent captain, and the right man for the job. The seeds were planted for a Welsh Grand Slam in 1971 and a brilliant Lions success in New Zealand.

Just for the record, I captained Wales thirteen times – six wins, three draws and four lost.

But now, in 1971 we were heading for a wonderful era. Every day was exciting and success snowballed. When you are playing well and expecting to win, then luck goes with you. The England Selectors helped us off the mark. They sent a team which included seven new caps to Cardiff! We all knew about Rossborough, the Coventry full back. He was rather 'delicate' under the high ball, so we let him have it. We practised it hard beforehand, Barry and I kicking, Arthur Lewis smashing in on the catcher, and John Dawes lurking in a support position to pick up the pieces. Gerald Davies actually scored from this situation, so there was a satisfaction and confidence about the team as we went to Scotland. Planning was paying off.

That Murrayfield match is now a famous moment in sport. I thought we had blown it! It was all right to keep telling ourselves that we were scoring the tries and Scotland were only getting penalty goals, but the addition worked out the same. Scotland were winning 18–14 and there were just four minutes left. 'That jammy beggar has done us,' I kept on saying about Peter Brown, because his penalty points had come from the most horrible-looking kicks, twirling, swirling, screwing and floating – all low and sneaking over the bar. Barry hit a post with a conversion, and mercifully Peter Brown did too after Chris Rea had scored the try which should have won the match. History now records that Wales made one last assault. Dawes was marvellous, as everyone recognized after the game. Knowing that there were just four minutes left after Chris Rea's try, he spread it about that we had ten minutes left including injury time.

It was Scotland's throw into a line-out on their own 25. The Scottish boys have since told me that Duncan Paterson first gave the wrong signal to his forwards. However, they had done so well in the line-out, he did not bother to change it. In came the ball, Delme Thomas won it with a superb hand-back to me. We spun the ball out to Gerald Davies as fast as we could; we got the overlap and away he went, curving around to the corner and making precious ground back in to the posts so that the conversion could be taken half way between touch and the posts. It was a fairy tale. Our emotions were drained already. No one had been more than four points in the lead from the start, and now it was 18–17 to Scotland.

When John Taylor, or Bas to us, took the conversion, I was standing with Delme Thomas. We had our backs to the posts. 'I can't look; just can't look, Gar,' he said.

'OK, Del. I'll look . . . here he goes . . . c'mon Bas you beauty . . . it's a good kick . . . they're cheering . . . he's bloody well done it Del. We've won . . . that's it . . . the whistle . . . it's all over. What a game!'

The field was instantly full of toilet rolls, flags, people. The world stood still. I was honestly staggered to think that this was another finish I had played so often by the lamp-post at home in Gwaun-cae-Gurwen. But in those days, if I had to go in for tea, I would always get back out to take a conversion or force a late try before my Mam called me in for the night. But this, is Murrayfield; this is where it was destined to happen. I never saw that in my dreams. I never saw Bas as the hero either, because he was twice the hero I had ever imagined. Here was a man who did not kick a great deal, but was left-footed and had a curl and a drift about his kicks from left to right which could draw them between the posts from the right hand side of the field. That is why he got the kick. But he only had once chance. Street football is dreamland. This was more than a kick. It was the character of the man. John Taylor did it, and no one can ever take it away from him.

When we cooled down we did think a bit about Scotland. It takes two teams to make a game like that. Frank Laidlaw said to me later, 'Gareth, I knew we wouldn't win even when we were 18–14 up. I knew it in my bones. There was just something about it I can't explain.'

As for our coach. We threw Clive Rowlands, fully clothed, into the tub. He hardly knew where he was: he just cried like a baby and confessed . . . he hadn't seen the final kick at all.

Ireland were beaten fair and square 23–9 at Cardiff, and in one of the fastest games of my life we beat France in Paris 9–5. Against Ireland we attacked like kings, and in Stade Colombes we tackled harder than ever before.

By this time I was going well. I got two tries against Ireland, and in France finished off that marvellous move sparked off by J. P. R. Williams from defence. John ran along way down the left touch. He drew the defence perfectly by looking inside at Denzil Williams and set me away on the touch side for a run to the corner. Wales were playing like true champions. We were swamped by a wave of hero worship. The angry voices from Penarth on a cold wet Monday evening were not to be heard; at least only as faint warnings in the back of my mind. Now there were hangers-on hanging on to hangers-on! That was fine as long as they did not attach themselves to me. I had decided to make my friends slowly, and out of rugby have come the best friends anyone could have in the world. Recognizing them was the problem at this stage. There were plenty of splendid imitations around.

I must make it clear that not only Wales, but every home international country had improved in team preparation and technique by the time the Lions were due in New Zealand in 1971. It was the first time that we had got everything right – talent, method, management and coaching. It was one of the sweetest experiences of a lifetime. I have only space here for a few reflections on New Zealand rugby, and, although I have started with mention of the brightest moment, I must be honest and say that we had become accustomed to losing. That is almost the same as going into each match without a chance. Success snowballs; so does defeat.

Wales have always come second to the All Blacks, and I never appeared in a Welsh side which beat New Zealand. They were all hard matches; if I were to make excuses I would say that there were crucial turning-points in each game which we might have avoided, and also we were caught mainly at points of transition and rebuilding ... except that is, the Welsh tour to New Zealand in 1969. I am glad I mentioned those two factors, but there is no way I am going to stand up and say that we were robbed.

Rugby football means so much to both our countries. When I have toured out there the crowds flock to airports, hotels, training sessions and of course to the matches. The newspapers were always full of rugby comment. Win or lose, we retained a huge following through our tours.

I have written before that the All Blacks of 1967 were popular and a fine lot after the matches. Unfortunately the 1972–3 players left a bad taste in the mouth. There were bad characters in the party whose strong voice overpowered the management. Children were not just refused autographs by the All Blacks, they were abused and brushed aside.

It was therefore delightful to have the old agreement to play hard against each other but to drink a few beers together re-established by Andy Leslie's boys. We still did not win, but at least the All Blacks showed how it is important to win well in a sporting way.

Along the line there were so many players I admired. When I was part of the World XV in South Africa in 1977, I thoroughly enjoyed getting to know three of the great forwards, Norton, Sutherland and Kirkpatrick. I began to understand so much more about New Zealanders and their rugby after chatting to them.

Of course Syd Going was a brilliant scrum-half. I never got to know him well because he was not forthcoming after matches. He kept himself to himself, but I respected his playing qualities. I suppose he came out on the better side more often than I did. He was an ideal player for the All Black forward style, a good kicker, quick passer and the famous Maori side-step!

For passing as an art I have to recall Chris Laidlaw. He was a fabulous passer but, come to think of it, I do not believe I ever saw a poor scrum-half or outside-half in a side around New Zealand.

Brian Lochore's presence can never be forgotten either. What a magnificent forward; what a superb leader. How wrong his selectors were to bring him back into the Test side in 1971 when he had more or less finished. As with Hannes Marais in South Africa, they should not do that sort of thing to great players. Lochore responded as everyone would to the hour of need, but it was like putting a thumb into a wall when the water was gushing out. Colin Meads, another great forward, was left in a similar situation when he was made captain against the 1971 Lions. Meads was mellowing. He had seen through an era of crushing All Blacks success before it came apart first in South Africa and then at home against us. Losing hurt Colin Meads, but after the Tests he was in amongst us, learning how to lose, clapping everyone on the back, swilling the beer. He carried it off better than many a winning captain, but I felt he deserved a better end.

There were so many superb All Blacks — Fergie McCormack, Peter Whiting and that nice, knowledgeable man, a terrific opponent, Ken Gray.

Touring New Zealand is hard, and some of the public make it harder. They share with Wales the distinction of having the biggest rugby bores in the world. In the players' language they are called 'heavies'. Add continual rain to that, and an All Black pack bearing down on you, and you will appreciate that a trip down under takes a lot out of you. It took a long rest to get it back.

By 1977 the All Blacks were rampant again and running the ball easily along the backs. I am glad they won that way. Their game often loses that dimension. Winning is the thing; and they are the most formidable when their sights are set on it.

I I

Of Scots and Irish and good ole English

I must be excused for not remembering every detail of every game. I will not make it up either. It is best, I think, to recall people and places and the stories about them.

Let's start with Edinburgh. My visits there, as at every other Home International base, involved little more than a couple of nights' stay: a bed in the North British Hotel, a stroll down Princes Street and a battle at Murrayfield. Players are not tourists. They are not up in Scotland for a few pints and a look around. They follow a schedule of official requirements and grab their pleasures as they can, late on Saturday night.

However, the players are certainly the centre of attraction, on and off the field. Life in the North British reaches almost siege proportions sometimes. I have often looked down on the large foyer from the first floor balcony and laughed at the sheer variety of Welshmen who find themselves shoulder to shoulder, tipping beer over each other, and shoving as if they had been told that the game had been transferred from Murrayfield on Saturday afternoon, to the lounge bar of the North British on Friday night.

Trying to mix with the crowds in order to have a chat with a genuine friend is almost impossible. Their questions are always the same. Total strangers come up and whisper intimately: 'All the best now boys. Don't let us down and don't come 'ome if you don't win.' Better still, 'Now look 'ere boys. We 'aven't come all this way to see you lose, especially as Dai 'ere is supposed to be at work ... well, 'e clocked in anyway. 'E's on the longest bloody shift in the 'istory of the tinplate industry, aren't you Dai?'

The Welsh team often goes to a cinema on the Friday night. Sometime after eleven o'clock one or two of the boys would have a night-cap and a sandwich. I remember finding a quiet corner of the lounge one Friday night with Barry John. Barry had stopped playing by that time. Everyone was eyeing us and eventually one short, red-faced patriot, who was wrapped around in a red-and-white scarf like a snake dancer by his python, could keep it in no longer. 'Hey. What the hell are you doing up at this time, Gareth? Barry, mun, let the boy go to bed. We've got to beat them Scots.' He turned quickly, because he had said his piece right from the heart. No Welshman could cope with failure on Friday night. But he tripped over Derek Quinnell's leg. 'Not you as well Derek. Duw. Take it easy boys, *bach*, beer an' all,' ... and that was that. Another Welshman had unloaded his chapel guilt perhaps. There was no need, we all had enough of that to go around!

Or quainter still, Gerald Davies and I were window-shopping in a shoe shop along Princes Street. Another red-and-white vision ever so casually eased his way up to us. He edged closer, determined to get some words in because all his mates were standing and staring a few yards away. He shuffled about, coughed and then nodded when he caught our eyes. 'Up for the match are you boys?' he blurted out.

Well honestly, what was the answer? – 'No, we've come to buy shoes.' The other favourite chatter before the Scottish game is the 'bogey'. 'Remember '51,' they all say. I can honestly say that I never once gave a thought in Edinburgh to what had happened to the Welsh side that long ago. Fear of the bogey-man was strictly for the fans and the press. It was like a conversation I had at Twickenham once with four Taffs who were hammering home the myth of the Twickenham 'swirl'. It was no use telling them that I had never seen the swirl and did not believe it at all.

I would not care to count the number of Welshmen who make the trip up north. I heard of a competition in Princes Street called 'Spot the jock'.

They all do the Princes Street ritual. Mind you, we go out there for a laugh. The tide of red and white rolls towards us. There are fifty conversations ahead, at least. 'Think you'll win?' or, 'Going to 'ave a go today, Gar?' or just, 'All right butty?' and a wink. That is if you can see the wink behind a life-size teddy bear wearing a kilt and playing the bagpipes. Whatever do the kids at home make of these jumbo peace-offerings?

I loved the coach trip to the ground at Murrayfield. It is unique. It is not far from Princes Street and the North British to Murrayfield, but it is through the city, pavements and roadsides overflowing with people going to the game. So the rugby gladiators make their way through the crowds to the arena.

Then when you have snaked through the people, Murrayfield presents itself, solid, square, organized. The dressing-rooms are spacious at the back of the stands. You cannot hear the crowds from there. Gerry Lewis was soon busy on his massage tables and I passed on my usual tidings to him, 'If you pack up today, Gerry, I'm going with you.' Off the dressing-room is a huge communal bath – the one into which Clive Rowlands was 'helped' fully-clothed, after John Taylor's conversion in 1971 – pegs all around the room so that there is plenty of space for the boys. The same old Scots officials used to come to say hello. They always seemed to be gentlemen up there. Then, when the time was come, it was out of the dressing-room, just a short walk through a corridor, and on to the field to the sound of pipes.

I could breathe at Murrayfield because it has long sloping terraces on three sides, and just one grandstand.

I always had the impression that the Scots were old fashioned. They are certainly a very proud nation but also, I felt, set in their ways. Right is right and wrong is wrong. They find compromise a painful experience. This extends to the law of rugby football. For Scotsmen, the law is the law and that's that.

In coaching development the Welsh Rugby Union moved faster. We had a coach, but Scotland called their coach an advisor. Wales handed out new jerseys to its players for every match and a pair of shorts and socks for the season. If they were torn, there was no trouble in replacing them. The Scotsmen hung on to the last vestiges of what they saw as true amateurism. They were tougher with their players over kit. They resented our coaching move at the start; they almost suggested that our victories were hollow because we had applied ourselves and had taken time to organize our efforts. I think they still eye us as if we are professionals; the Welsh players are getting paid. I was never ever paid either by Cardiff or Wales.

I did respect Scotland for their resolution and indeed they have moved too. They set up their advisor and coaching week-ends. They even went ahead of other countries by organizing league tables. They were never afraid of issues.

Saturday nights in Edinburgh, win or lose, were always great fun. The security surrounding an offical Scottish RFU dinner was immaculate. Getting into one was like breaking into Fort Knox; getting out was just about the same. The committee men on both sides enjoy themselves and so they should. I am not one of those who criticize the Unions for giving their voluntary helpers a night out with their wives. I think they deserve it. The business of charging around local clubs in your area as their representative is chore enough in the winter nights.

One Saturday night in Edinburgh after the dinner I was sitting with J.P.R., Syd Millar and Andy Irvine. We had a touch of champagne, and the manager, understanding the situation, let us sit in the dining-room to get out of everyone's way. It was just off the ball-room; a little peace and quiet for a few memories. All of a sudden there was a clatter and a rumble at the window behind us. In jumped a taff. He was not exactly as quiet as a cat burglar, but he had certainly cracked the famous Scottish security. In a flash he had his jacket off on the floor out of sight, picked up a table cloth, folded it up, put it over his arm, the perfect wine waiter! He said he had posed as Clive Rowlands at the door but got thrown out. He did not last too long at the ball, but at least he made it, and that made his trip. In fact he came up to me a long while later introducing himself as 'the bloke who came in over the window when you and J.P.R. were having a drink'.

Perhaps I did manage to smuggle a friend into one dinner in Edinburgh. J. J. Williams came to me and said, 'There's a fella outside the function who says he wants to see you.' J.J. could not remember his name. I thought it could be anybody, a real 'heavy' perhaps, so I prepared to ignore it. 'Oh! and he said to give you this Gar,' J.J. just remembered. In his hand was a sea-trout tube fly. It could only be Graham Evans, my fishing pal from Swansea. There was no way I could stand the buffeting in the public rooms if I went to talk to him there, so I took off my bow-tie, slipped it first into my pocket and gave it to Graham when I met him. In no time he presented himself to the doorman in black-tie, I went guarantor and that was that. He was in. For the rest of the night we spent hour after hour listening to Charlie Drummond, lapping up the delicacies of fishing on Scottish waters. Magic. The disappointment of losing to Scotland that day eased away.

The only opportunity of making real friends of play-ers from other countries is to do a Lions tour together. Even then there are thirty or so members of the party and it very much depends on your leisure interests as to how much time you spend in each others' company. One Scottish friendship was all too brief. Jock Turner was a Lion of '68 in South Africa. We got on well and he always looked me up after his playing days or rang up when I was in Scotland.

I must retell one particular experience with Jock. It was just after Wales had returned from their agony tour of New Zealand in the summer of 1969. I drove Maureen up to Scotland for a holiday. I did not know exactly where I was going, but Jock Turner was always the sort of man to say, even if he had a full house and I had an army of people with me, 'Fine, clear the garage, we've got friends coming.' That is what I did: I called on Jock.

Out in his Scottish countryside he treated me to fishing, shooting, the lot, and we drank beer with the passion of two trench pals, reunited after war. 'Remember South Africa '68? It was hell, but we were there.' And we are back . . . sort of feeling.

One night, after we had downed a few pints, I had the crazy idea that I had better keep in training for the season ahead. You know how logic leaves you at that point? It was midnight. A lot of pints had been shifted when I said, 'Jock, we had better run this lot out.'

On went the track suits, and off we pounded. It could have killed us. We were mad. What a sight, on a pitch-black morning in July. Chatting, running, stopping to be sick.

In the morning we went out in disbelief to measure the distance we had run. The route we had taken was straight into the country; there could have been no help.. The distance . . . four and a half miles!

Of other Scotsmen I recall Roger Arneil, tall, fairheaded. He was modest, perhaps doubting his own ability at the start, but a magnificent British Lion. Originally, in 1968, he was not chosen for the Lions tour. Then England's Brian West withdrew during the warm-up sessions at Eastbourne. In came Roger, disbelieving, training his guts out, making himself ill after games because his heart had gone so deeply into his efforts. He had a lot to offer, but more the grit and devotion than the finesse of a John Taylor. He was hard, but he was clean. We got on well. When he came out to the Lions tour of New Zealand in '71 as a replacement, he was still in very good shape and form and played for Scotland until 1973.

We did once have cross words . . . shattering words which were my fault. Scotland were at Cardiff during the time when the changing facilities were temporary huts, and both teams were almost rubbing shoulders with each other. I was standing in the toilet have a pensive pee before the match, when a Scottish voice beside me said, 'How are you, Gareth! Good to see you. Good luck today.' It was Roger Arneil.

I glared and then growled and spat out something like, 'And you can get stuffed for a start you ———' I was off and away.

Apparently Roger was upset. I have regretted saying that to this day. I suppose it was part of my motivation, but it was so unneccesary. Afterwards I apologized and he insisted, 'No, you were right. This isn't a Lions tour. You had the right attitude. I was upset for twenty minutes of that game.' Right or wrong, given another chance to answer that gentle inquiry after my health, I would have chosen few but different, more generous words.

Golf was always an attraction to me on tour, and that is where Gordon Brown and I made our friendship. Broon of Troon was a fine tourist. Certainly by 1974 he could look after himself as well as any of the hardest international forwards in the world. He became a cornerstone of the Lions side. He was well liked by every team.

He would do anything for a good game of golf, so you can imagine his reaction to an invitation from Gary Player to play along with Mike Gibson and me. Broonie, however, was injured. His hand was painful; there was no way he could grip the club. Yet the big man virtually demanded a pain-killing injection from the doctor in order to take up this offer of a lifetime. (It must have been fairly unique for Gary Player too!)

Yes, we were great mates, but again the Edwards

Welsh-terrier temperament almost lost him a pal. Let me set the scene. 1974 Scotland versus Wales at Murrayfield. Scotland dropped out of their 25. The ball went too far ahead of their forwards and reached me. As I took it Broonie was up there, ploughing all over me, fair but hard. Everyone fell on top of us. As the ruck formed I tried to get out but I was pinned down by a Scots forward in a disgusting way. He saw my leg sticking out of the mass of bodies and screwed his stud into it. I screamed like a stuck pig. He knew he was doing it. There was a bloody great hole in my leg afterwards.

I got to my feet mad, blind mad, going around in circles for revenge. The ball by now was a good forty yards away and I limped off towards the play. But I saw a blue shirt on the floor near me. I ran to him. It was Broonie. 'Who was it? Who was it?' I spat out. Suddenly I let fly my hardest punch. Whack! 'Take that you bastard,' I screamed, and cracked him in the face. It was almost as if time stood still.

I can see Broonie's eyes going wide with disbelief, and as he recovered the power of speech he simply wailed, 'What d'y want t'do that for?'

'Aw. Shut-up,' I chirped back. 'You're the only bloke left, so I had to hit you.' How is that for Welsh logic!

I had hit him as hard as I could but all he did as we followed the play to the next line-out was grin, 'Is it safe here?' I suppose I hardly touched him . . . I hope so, anyway.

That evening a Scottish player offered the information, 'It wasn't Broonie who did it, it was me.' I did not want to know him; nor have I forgiven him.

Bobby Windsor was on hand, listening in. All he said was, 'You'll be sorry for that if you're around at Cardiff next year.'

I hope by exclusion no one north of the Border thinks that they have been less than good sportsmen. I am simply throwing in a few anecdotes to bring back the memories. How can I ever forget Frank Laidlaw – not especially because he was such a pleasant man, but

because he was the first hooker I had ever seen hooking
the ball with his head! Myburgh, the massive South
African prop, was crippling the Welsh prop Barrie
Llewelyn. The Babas front row was locked with all
heads to the ground. Frank told me to aim the ball for
his head not his feet when I fed the scrum. I did. He
nodded it back, no trouble at all. I've seen Bob Windsor
do the same thing since, but there is nothing quite like
seeing it done for the first time.

I recall sharing a room with Frank on a Lions tour.
The light was on. I was reading, Frank was sleeping.
What do you do when your roomy screams in the middle of the night, 'C'mon Stack, pundi, pundi. Pundi,
pundi Stack. Good man Stack pundi, pundi.' Frank
cries. I knew that forwards were a different race but
that was ridiculous. You see, when the Scots wanted
weight in the scrummage they would call out for extra
poundage, 'Pundi, pundi'. That's what it sounded like.
Stack Stevens was the loose-head forward of course, and
it looked as if he and Frank were scrummaging against
New Zealanders all night as well as all day. Must have
been a hard tour for them, keeping the shove on for
twenty-four hours a day!

We laughed at that, and indeed Frank was a delightful man. In later days he asked me more than once to
go up to Scotland to play in matches for his own special
charity. If I regretted not being able to do anything it
was that. Now that the pressure is off, I would like to
help if I can.

Good rugby players those Scots – Mighty Mouse
McLauchlan, Sandy Carmichael, Broonie of course,
Roger Arneil and Jim Telfer, the unknown. Nice lads
those scrum-halves, Paterson, McCrae, Morgan and all;
the talented McGeechan and the brilliant Andy Irvine.
Irvine playing in a side with settled half-backs, as
Wales have had over a long period, would have been
even more superb. I hope that is not heresy.

Off the field there is always George Burrell to take me
fishing, Doug Smith to ask me if my hamstring troubles

are still 'in the mind', or rather pointing to my head and asking, 'How are yer hamstrings? Still up there in yer arse?' Doug Smith and Carwyn James were a fine combination of coach and management in 1971 in New Zealand. 'Bagpipes' Smith was very approachable and pleasant, but firm when needed. Between them they did a lot for the image of British rugby. But, there you are, when the Lions aircraft set down at Heathrow, and the farewells had been said, and the promises made, my car still sped down the M4 to Wales, the Scots flew on to Scotland, and the next bagpipes I heard were in my ears when I took the field in a red jersey again to call 'em rotten before the match and drink 'em under the table after it. I had a simple formula.

So to Lansdowne Road. Ireland is fair, but Ireland is furious. I am first of all grateful to Ireland for beating Wales at Cardiff in 1967. They paved the way for my first cap. I was a gloating onlooker. I have never lost my respect for the Irish for the way in which they always contested every match, although they almost ended my international career at Dublin in 1970. That time they put the curse of the leprechaun on my performance. First sight of my great friend Roger Young was across the table in Ireland in '68. The Lions tour was our objective. He had been on the Lions tour of 1966. Was he going to be in my way, or might I go to South Africa with him? I treated him, like any novice should, with suspicion and Edwards hate. Soon we were inseparable allies.

The Irish win over Wales in 1970 gave them all the revenge they needed for the Brian Price-Murphy affair the previous year. We stayed out of town at the Green Isle Motel. We were disappointed but had just begun to laugh again as I was getting my kit together to leave the bus and go off to my room. One of the Welsh Selectors, who shall remain 'brainless', said, 'I don't know what you are laughing about; I don't think you'll be in the next team.'

I shot back at him as a man wounded by leading an unsuccessful attempt to win the Triple Crown in Ireland, 'Right. Let me know quickly; the fishing season starts next week and I want to know whether to buy a licence or not.'

It was a terrible statement for a selector to make at that moment. Obviously he had never played rugby at that level. We were just recovering from our own post mortem on the bus and had accepted that defeat boiled down to our own mistakes. That was that; now for the dinner at the Hibernian.

Irish dinners are marvellous. They all seemed to happen in a little back room; no magnificent decor, just an old guy playing the honky-tonk piano in the corner and a good old fashioned get-together. All the players used to sit on one table: I liked that. The pints of ale went down well on that occasion, and we enjoyed the fun before facing the press the next day.

There was great warmth to be felt in the company of Willie John McBride, who puffed away on his pipe, peaceful, looking smaller then than on the field. 'How is Bancyfelin?' he used to ask after his old mate Delme Thomas, the retired big Welsh lock forward who lived in the West Wales village of Bancyfelin. McBride always sat quietly in a corner, like the sheriff in a western film. But as soon as the baddies arrived he would be in there, up to his armpits. I suppose he was the John Wayne of rugby football, even down to his slow words and heavy movements.

He was my sort of captain. In South Africa in 1974 I would have followed him anywhere. Willie would not rant and rave in his team talks. I can see him now, bent forward, addressing the team which was hushed around him. 'There is no escape.' That was it with Willie John, his creed of total commitment. In his mind it was high noon again: lay down your life or don't come with me; follow me over the top. 'I hate small men,' I often heard him say.

Yes, this is the Willie John of pranks and parties too.

I remember as a wide-eyed youngster, how I watched him sink a bottle of brandy, and a bottle of whisky with Peter Stagg, in South Africa '68. We left them to it, but later Willie arrived at another party with a bottle of Dry Cane under his arm. We never expected to see him again that night, let alone standing up. He steadied his John Wayne stance in the doorway, feet wide apart, and just drawled, 'I've just see that Stagg away,' – as easy as if he had popped out to put the car in the garage!

Of course, by the time he came to captain the Lions he too had matured a lot since '68. Many things had changed since those boisterous days. Now, here was a man of vast experience who never wasted words, always worth listening to, and always with a good song to sing.

He was respected on the field. He never turned the other cheek. If someone was rough with Willie they knew that he would compete, but I never saw him sacrifice the team's performance because of some niggle or other. He would prefer to win. I remember leading Wales, again in Ireland (you see the sort of jobs I had), in 1974. There were some fierce exchanges from both sides and about four or five boys were left lying on the ground holding their heads, writhing in pain The only Irishman down was tying up his bootlace, that's all. The referee then gave a penalty to Ireland for dangerous play. I was going mad, storming at the referee. Willie John came over, cool and collected. 'Yes,' the referee was saying, 'a dangerous tackle.'

I turned to Willie and screamed, just as I had screamed at Broonie before, 'Right, if that's the way you want it, you'll have it.' Ray McLoughlin was standing by solid, square-jawed, flat-nosed. 'The same goes for you too,' I shouted clenching my fist. He tugged his old scrum-cap straight and smiled. Typical Edwards; typical McBride; typical McLoughlin.

In the dinner that night Ray was the first up to me to say, 'Now tell me, Gareth. That wasn't you t'reatening me out there today was it?' They both knew they could have murdered me without anyone seeing it happen . . .

if they could have caught me.

Yes, Willie John McBride was respected by his troops. Again I see him in team talks before Test matches in South Africa in '74, puffing the pipe, then slowly raising a bent finger to sum up the whole discussion. 'Just remember lads. There is no retreat. No more talk now; just make peace with yourselves.'

By the end of the third Test against those Springboks we were carrying him off the field, the series won for Britain, and he sat in his corner of the dressing-room and said simply what it meant to him. 'Gar, I can now die happy,' . . . and Willie John was no man of idle promises. Let me emphasize this spirit of total commitment, all for one and one for all, which was very much McBride's law.

Phil Bennett had hurt his leg after the second Test in that series. It was a nasty gash which he sustained as he made a brilliant infield break to score a brilliant and priceless try. Now, many ignorant people, even press critics, have questioned Benny's guts, but I can tell you that he was no 'jacker'. He stayed on the field that afternoon, even though the doctor told him to go off. The cut eventually needed about twelve stitches. Willie John knelt over him, 'C'mon Benny, I need you.' That was enough. My partner stayed where he was and finished the game.

The day after the Test we went off to relax in the Kruger Park. Benny had come with us even though he could not walk. However, wherever he went Willie John carried him around on his back, and we all knew why.

Late that evening there were about eight of us sitting in a circle. The night was dark but warm. We sipped beers as Willie John sang away in sweet Irish notes, *Scarlet Ribbons*. We were a long way from home; we had won the war; we were a team together.

The beer was going down well in rather large quantities when suddenly we heard voices. Another British Lions party was making its way up the hill towards us and we caught their conversation. 'C'mon lads,' someone said, 'we'll go up and throw them out of bed.'

We were billeted in *rondavels*, small round safari huts. Instinctively everyone got up and rushed away to their own quarters. It was a case of 'Let's get the hell out of here and barricade ourselves in.' Willie John picked up Benny again and threw him on his back. We rushed down one of the darkest paths. Imagine how, when we came to a *rondavel*, we had to feel blindly for the outline of the numerals on the door to find out if we had arrived home. In pitch-dark and homeless, the captain and his little soldier beat their way through the trees until, whack, a low branch suddenly knocked Benny off Willie's back. If ever there was an injustice! Just as well they were fairly relaxed! Benny re-mounted and disappeared. We could not find them again. They must have got to safety we thought, but no one knew for certain.

It was in the sober morning that everyone asked the question about their health and whereabouts. Had they found their beds? Then one of the boys called me. Come and see this, he said. I followed him into Willie's *rondavel* and there I saw the giant fast asleep, his frame only just contained by the single bed. It was just like a school bed, grey blanket and all, and there tucked in the crook of his arm, like a little baby . . . Benny, soundly asleep; protected by the man for whom he had given so much the day before at Loftus Versveld.

What else of the Irish? I shall always remember the sheer science of Ray McLoughlin's scrummaging. He was hard as well, with wide shoulders. I saw him handle a Waikato prop in New Zealand as if he was a piece of inanimate substance to be shifted up and down on a car jack. Ray just slotted the poor man into whatever cog he wanted – you could almost hear the ratchet clicking through the poor man's vertebrae.

Syd Millar was first the hard prop and later the motivator of a coach in 1974. There were again people who wrote him off as being a disciple only of kick and rush tactics. In 1974 I was delighted how thoughtful he was. He was prepared to listen and give out the rein, as well as pull you in.

Then there was Fergus Slattery, one of the world's best open-side wing forwards. He was a 'put-another-battery-in' type of player. Non-stop. In that Welsh match in Dublin in 1978 he did go over the top, throwing his boot in all directions, but that was oddly un-Slattery. He was a better player than that.

As I have said, I always appreciated the skills of Mike Gibson. I naturally looked up to him as a senior Lion when I first toured. He helped me so much with those old passing problems, just by his understanding. He probably would have liked more of the ball from me, but my game was immature and more a solo effort in those days.

Mike never drank alcohol, though he did stomach a little champagne on my twenty-first birthday. A golf-lover, but generally did his own thing on tour, an independent soul. The strength of his play was his preparation, which was dedicated and strenuous and his ability on the field to sum up situations on the move. He could persuade an opponent to pass the ball at a time that suited us. He could tackle like a demon when physical presence was required. His basic skills were model. The combination of strength and vision made him one of the best players to play with, and one of the most feared to oppose. His performance for the Lions in New Zealand in 1971 was one of the high points of centre-three-quarter play during my whole career.

Of Roger Young, Ken Goodall and Tom Kiernan elsewhere. All I can say to them all, and apologies for omissions – I am relieved that entry to heaven does not hinge on a Welsh victory in Dublin, because I would be an even bet to end up in warmer climes!

Just a few more words about France and the French, even though I have already painted a lot of colour in Paris when Wales have played there. The action is all red-and-white scarves, cognac and a struggle with the language. On the field, referees find the language a problem, though I do remember George Burrell's brother, R. P. Burrell refereeing Wales and France in Paris in 1969. He had obviously worked hard at his French, although it was delivered in a rich Scots accent. He came out with warning to the *'taloneur Français'*, and lots of rugby phrases like that. That's the hooker. At one scrum I was having touble with the put-in. After a couple of attempts he tapped me on the shoulder wagged his finger and said, *'Voulez-vous mettre le ballon au milieu, s'il vous plaît?'*

I could only laugh back, 'Good grief, try it in Welsh mate, give me a bit of a chance.'

The French rugby players are hard, talented and highly organized on the field as well as generous and jovial off it. They live life with a bit of flourish, and after an international match not only their current players will take you under a wing and give you a good time, but old internationals come up with ageing smiles and million-doller handshakes to offer you a club, restaurant or whatever you like.

Michel Pebeyre comes to mind, a big strapping boy, whom I first met in opposition when a Welsh team played the Welsh Rugby Union's President's XV to celebrate the opening of the new ground, the National Stadium, at Cardiff Arms Park. Throughout my career, as I have mentioned, one of my hobbies was collecting rugby balls after the game, and I had a bit of luck this time, because play ended with the ball in my hands. The President's ball would be a lovely memento of the day when we first saw Welsh rugby in its smart, new setting.

Thundering footsteps sounded behind me. Michel Pebeyre had done a thirty-yard sprint with the same idea in mind. He just stood and looked at me with sad old eyes, 'Oh. Gareth!' That's all he said. I just had to give the ball to him. It would have been cruelty to deny him. He had not been capped by France at that time, and I thought it might be the biggest day of his life.

Next year Wales went to Paris for the Grand Slam and won it. During the evening Michel Pebeyre turned up. He was not playing, though he had been capped, and, in fact, was destined to be in the French team against me in Paris in 1973. 'I have come for you, Gareth. You were kind to me in Cardiff. You gave me the match ball. Tonight you are my guest. Bring your friend with you.'

So Barry John and I joined them in a gleaming Rolls Royce. Jo Maso was with us too and away we went into their favourite Paris haunts, club to club. A great night. I remember going eventually to a club called Winston Churchills, having noticed an advertisement outside for English beer. We barged in and there serving behind the bar were J.P.R. and Mervyn Davies. They had taken over. 'What do you want, Gar?' J.P.R asked.

'Gin and tonic,' I said.

Whoosh! a bottle of gin appeared on the bar from nowwhere. 'Help yourself,' he said.

I recall, too, walking back to the hotel very early in the morning. We had won the Grand Slam and I never wanted it to end; I wanted to savour it, never to go to bed. With me was Ken Kennedy, the Irish hooker, though I'm not sure what he was doing there. Very special those French boys, we agreed. Win or lose they enjoy themselves, and what a way to fête a Grand Slam – coasting around Paris in a Rolls with a bunch of lads who, as Michel Pebeyre proved, do not forget.

The French have a taste for night-clubs when the hard business of rugby is over. It was after a bruising match in Paris in 1976 when Wales lost that Jean-Pierre Rives set off on the town with Phil Bennett, J.P.R., J.J. and me in tow. The French Federation always take over a night-club and the drinks are free to players. Outsiders can get in too, but they buy their own.

J. J. Williams happened to be leaning against the bar but rather than walk through the crowd for free drinks he offered to buy beers for Nigel Starmer-Smith and me. 'Go to the free bar, J.J.,' I said, laughing because he was always thought to be a bit 'protective' of his money. 'No, I'm going to buy you boys a beer,' he insisted. It was going to be the generous J.J. tonight. He delivered the beers and picked up the bill . . . £11!

Jean-Pierre a superb host took us from night-club to night-club, free champagne all the way. Phil Bennett stole the show in the early hours of the morning by insisting on singing to Sacha Distel at his dinner table. Why he chose, 'I'm going home to Swansea Town', I cannot think. He only knew the first line which he kept repeating and, worse still, he lives in Llanelli. I must compliment Sacha Distel. He was most tolerant and polite.

Eventually we decided to retreat to the hotel. However, as our car drew up outside, we spotted half a dozen Welsh supporters, still swathed in their red-and-white scarves and looking as if they had taken the defeat rather badly. Our reaction was not to be seen because they would probably tell the world that we were out all night, up to no good.

Jean-Pierre insisted that it was all right. The car stopped, he threw open the door, put one foot in the gutter and was suddenly violently sick. Cheers from the Welsh brigade. 'They may have beaten us at rugby, Gareth, but they can't hold their bloody drink, can they?'

Poor Jean-Pierre could not win.

England were the enigmas in my playing days. They were always hard to beat because they deprived us of so much ball, but somehow they could never put their whole game together.

It was inbred in us, of course, from a young age to say to ourselves, 'We've got to beat the English; we've got to beat the English.' I think the long succession of Welsh wins made us even more suspicious of them. 'Is this their year? They are due to smash us. I hope they leave it another year so that I can be out of the way.'

That was the sort of feeling. Losing to England was unthinkable.

Maybe the followers of rugby football did not think England's chances were very high, but I knew how good their players were. On Lions tours I had seen boys of talent and guts. John Pullin was a world-class hooker and loose forward, Tony Neary another outstanding player. I could never understand why Tony failed to hold his England place after the Lions tour of 1974. Peter Wheeler is another forward who would have won a place in any country's side . . . Fran Cotton, Roger Uttley and so many others. To my amazement, the results never came their way, and because of my affection for them on tour, I used to feel sorry for them in the evening after England–Wales matches. That sounds silly but it is true. I used to look at Fran Cotton, remember how much he had done for Britain abroad, how much stick he had taken, how much he knew about the game and how superb he was technically, and think that he must have felt he was living a nightmare every year in an English jersey.

The analysts could always argue that victory went to Wales by the thickness of a post, or by the gust of a freak wind, but the story was always the same at the end. When it came to the nitty-gritty, it was always Wales who had taken her chances.

Geographically England's administration has its problems. In Wales our selectors can see us play three times a week if they want. We are tightly knit, and comparisons between players are easier to make. Inbred in the many English counties is a diversity of thinking. How can rugby players who are city workers in London feel the same about rugby as a handful of farmers from Devon? Or perhaps a more revealing question – where does rugby football stand in their daily life? In Wales it is the staple diet. It is not in England. I've said that David Duckham and Peter Wheeler can walk down the main street in Cardiff and be recognized by almost everyone they pass. It would not happen to them to that extent in Coventry or Leicester their home cities. Men used to losing never expect to win. The appetite for soaking up pressure only comes when you know you can endure it and win in the end. So often Wales have been behind on points and have come back as if it was their destiny. The difference of local approaches in English rugby is obvious in the county championship. In Wales country rugby is a non-entity. It is useful only to see promising youngsters have a go, or to reward a stalwart of the club game who has come close to a cap but never made it. But England is different, and I recall making a mistake about underestimating their county loyalties.

It was in Lancashire. I was the after-dinner speaker at the function which celebrated Lancashire's county championship win. I tried to make it a jokey occasion with lots of Welsh anecdotes and funny stories. Afterwards Tony Neary, whom I had not met before, told me that I has mis-read the occasion. I was new and a bit nervy, but a few days later I could see he was right. I should have delved into the tradition of the county game. As Tony said, 'There are young boys here whose greatest achievement in a life-time is to win that title.' I was grateful to him for putting me right. I wish I had appreciated the mettle of the competition up in the north before I went there.

Since those days I have seen Barry Nelmes, the Gloucestershire and England prop, who played for Cardiff with me, work up a sweat at the prospect of a Gloucestershire match, and I have understood it.

However the system of county rugby can be quite treacherous to selectors. It is possible that the best centre-three-quarter in the country is playing in a bad side. He will never look as good as a man in a successful team. Maybe his club is not one of the tops either. All he needs is one bad international trial and he is as good as gone.

In Wales the selectors reach the trial stage knowing exactly who they want in the side. That is how it should always be. Much more emphasis can be placed on working out moves and coordinating the effort; using the trial as a dummy run.

It all comes back to the geographical variation. If I have had a bad Welsh trial I could always expect three or four Welsh selectors to be watching me during the week in a club match. Two chances are better than one.

I am not one who believes English players lack the *hwyl* or intensity. They should not be branded with the 'old-school-tie' image, though one or two of the committee do their best to prolong the old reputation of carefree rugby football without the results to match. The sort of men I respect are people like Eric Evans and Dickie Jeeps, two former captains who knew how to be successful on the field, and knew how to shake hands when the battle was over – win or lose.

One of the tales that made us laugh was of the RFU President who went into the England team dressing-room as they were changing before an international and called them to order. 'Just a moment, chaps. My wife would like a word with you.'

They stood there in disbelief as she said, 'I just wanted to come and see you, and to wish that you all do well.' Can you imagine Clive Rowlands being coach and allowing that to happen!

Let me also balance that by pointing to one of the enviable assets of English rugby. More Englishmen have got the game in proper perspective than Welshmen. The game is for winning, but it is for enjoyment. The element of physical exercise and a few pints afterwards should always exist at club level. I have seen the game in Wales even at minor club level destroy families. I have seen players crying, shouting or threatening when they lose. From the man in the street to the international players at the top there builds up a huge rugby pressure. Sometimes it is like a quicksand and we are sucked into endless rugby talk. Then, Welshmen are boring: the game is removed from its proper position in life. It eats us up.

I must talk about English three-quarters, and before

all others, two come to mind, David Duckham and John Spencer. At one stage they had almost the superstar image, the blond duo. The English press built them up, perhaps because they needed a couple of dashing heroes so badly. In the eventual killing-off of Duckham and Spencer the press, who had made them, were unforgivable. Some rugby writers have the dangerous notion that all the true judgement comes from off the field. John Spencer, particularly, was written out of the game.

When they went to New Zealand with the Lions in 1971 they were both playing well. Then, without any warning, John Spencer hit a strange crossroads. At Pukehohe in the first match he was forced to play on the wing because of injuries, and he missed three or four try-scoring opportunities. He was slated in the press.

He was obviously unsettled, but the boys encouraged him. After all he was not supposed to be a tearaway wing or even an electric hare of a centre. It was only an experiment. That was a day when even Barry John was slipping and sliding about. The playing surface was a mess. Anyway, the Lions worked about five overlaps in the match, but John Spencer only made it to the line once. We beat Counties and Thames Valley 25 points to 3.

Thereafter nothing much went right for John. The Test centres became John Dawes and Mike Gibson, and pushing them hard were Arthur Lewis and Chris Rea, Alistair Biggar and Dave Duckham, who also turned out in the centre. However amid all these playing problems there emerged a man whom everyone on that trip admired for his personal qualities. I've seen great players injured on Lions tours, or out of form and left out of Test teams, and they have been dragged down by their luck. They have been miserable, and spread their misery through the team.

Not John Spencer. He laughed and joked although his heart must have been bleeding. Injury hit him too, but he used his time keeping everyone's morale high. After all, if he was cheerful how could any of us dare be anything else?

He used to make up little poems. 'I'm not a pheasant plucker; I'm a pheasant plucker's son; When I'm not plucking pheasant . . .' and so on.

The following year at Cardiff I was tackled hard by none other than J. S. Spencer. He clung to me whispering as we went down to the bottom of a ruck, 'D'y'know, I'm not a pheasant plucker; I'm a pheasant plucker's son. . . .'

He became a specialist in Welsh societies in New Zealand. Almost everywhere we went there were invitations for the Welsh boys to meet the exiles. John loved to come with us and we taught him phrases in Welsh. He studied and practised them until he was near perfect. What he did not realize was that many of the sayings we taught him were rather rude! In translation the most decent of them came out as, 'How's you bum, missus?' or, 'How's your conkers?' In sailed John with his new language and thought that open mouths were signs of amazement at his excellence!

A few months later the last laugh went to Spencer. It was at a Welsh Valley town where the people of the town were fêting the Lions who had returned victorious. He immediately unleased his Welsh. From the look of the Mayoress's face it was the only time that anyone had greeted her with a handshake and, 'Shummae, how's your conkers?'

He could see it had misfired, so he quickly added, 'Gareth, Barry and Gerald taught me that.'

John never recovered the ground as a player after that tour. All I can tell him is that in Wales (Swansea Bay Golf Club to name just one place!) he always has the welcome reserved for very fine players and only the best sportsmen.

Dave Duckham was a different personality, far more intense and aggressive in his play. Sometimes I thought he was rather too intense before big games. Dave would be clenching his fist in the corner muttering, 'Come on boys, we've got to do it,' building himself up. I wanted him to relax because that is what his game needed. He too fell out of favour with the English selectors, but he was a world-class player. Possibly there were spells when he was below his very best, but he would always have been in my side. He went a long time without scoring a try for England. That is the fault of the team's performance not his. It was the same when Gerald Davies came back to Cardiff. He couldn't score tries. We decided that it was not his form, but our system that was wrong – and it was.

David Duckham certainly proved himself in the Welsh eye. Dai Duckham, Welsh folk called him. Blond, powerful, with a dummy and a side-step all his own. Like John Spencer, miracles were expected of him in an English jersey, but how could they produce them when England were never commanding enough at half-back?

Tony Neary is another who I think was underestimated as his career went on. Because he did not have a cauliflower ear and a flat nose, he tended to look like a film star more than an international forward. Yet he was a tough, unselfish and sensible footballer. There have been very few occasions when I have been truly sad to see someone left out of Lions Test matches – after all only fifteen can play. But Tony Neary and Fergus Slattery were inseparable in 1974 in South Africa. Slattery deserved to play too, but must have got it on the toss of a coin. They were superb. Certainly in 1978 the Welsh team which went to Twickenham were relieved to hear that Tony Neary was on the substitutes bench and not on the field.

Obviously I have a kaleidoscope of memories of rugby played against England, from my first game, Keith Jarrett's match in 1967, to the last tough 9–6 win at Twickenham in 1978. In the twelve matches I have played I was lucky enough to be on the losing side only once. I shall not forget the 11–11 draw in 1968 at Twickenham because of one special moment. The Welsh reserve scrum-half was British Lion Alan Lewis.

He was not a man of many words, but he had the modesty and decency to come up to me and say, 'Gareth, I really have to tell you, that today you had your best game for Wales.' Coming from a reserve with a lot of pride at stake, that was unforgettable. Aberavon's Bob Wanbon got a try in that match. It was a vital one to get the draw. So the first-ever Welsh team coach David Nash will be remembered for his comment in the dressing-room afterwards, but please don't judge him by that alone, 'Bobby,' he said. 'You may have scored, but you shouldn't have been standing in that position at all.' What a killer! Bob went north after that match. Yes, don't mistake me, David Nash was a nice man who knew his rugby. It was just an unfortunate comment which came out at the time. When I think how our front row and line-out were mangled by England on that day, I reckon it was a miracle that we drew.

Then to '69 and the Triple Crown match at Cardiff; hard match, but a comfortable win in the end, 30–9. The English full back at the time, R. B. Hiller of the Harlequins to me always looked pompous and aloof on and off the field. His Oxford background made it easy to believe first impressions. How wrong I was. What a great Lions tourist! What a superb kicker of the ball! What a trier! Like John Spencer, and others who have produced the bright side of their personalities when doomed to a reserve berth on tour, Bob Hiller was exceptional. In South Africa 1968 he was up against the tour captain Tom Kiernan; in 1971 in New Zealand against John Williams. He pushed them both and scored over 100 points on each tour. 'Boss' Hiller, as he was called by the lads, had all the subtleties of humour. Once he was preparing to kick at goal in New Zealand, taking his time to dig a large platform for the ball, and sizing up the posts. A fellow on the bank shouted, 'Do you want a shovel, Hiller?' Bob turned and picked him out in loud Oxford and Quins tones. 'Give me your mouth; that's big enough.' Boss turned, planted the ball, stepped ever so slowly back and then proceeded to take his deep breathing exercises. In he came and bang! The ball slowly revolved and like so many of his kicks set off like a remote control missile high between the posts. Boss turned and gave them a giant Harvey Smith.

Bob Hiller was far from aloof. He struck up a dazzling relationship with another reserve Chico Hopkins, the lad from Maesteg. They were from vastly different backgrounds but they worked out a repartee which was funny to everyone, usually based on Chico's dream one day 'to turn out for the 'Arlequins'.

In all the matches I played against England I met players of character and talent, too many to mention. Why then have England not been successful? Firstly, I believe that Wales confronted them with something special – advanced ideas on team preparation and outstanding individual talents. Yet I am always left asking myself year after year whether England had done the best they possibly could. Their forwards won enough ball to win almost all the matches. It is how they used it that decided the issues. I faced nine English scrum-halves in my time. Perhaps the best was Bill Redwood of Bristol. The English selectors of the day called on him to play his couple of representative games far too late in his career. Experience of the international field is so essential before you can truly express yourself and start to win a match or two.

Team-building is an art of sense and instinct. England's trip to Australia did not work because they chose too many youngsters. As injuries occurred they tried to patch things up with more experienced players, but they missed an opportunity of shaping a side for the future. A lot of these youngsters, Peter Kingston, Peter Knight and others were never seen again. Wales took a different attitude over their tour to Japan. They did not take Joe Bloggs of Cwmscwt. They jumped at the chance to build up team spirit, because only touring does that properly, and so developed a slightly changed side around the established players.

My last critical impression of England's rugby is that they appear to be confused about the approach behind the scrum. When they chose Martin Cooper, who was a runner, they sometimes gave him Lampkowski who, as a scrum-half, was a short passer. Then, when Cooper played with, say, Steve Smith, who could pass some distance, then Cooper played a kicking game. If a kicker was required then Alan Old should have been chosen who was best at that. Then again, the idea of moving the ball was held up in the centre where there were always defensive players short of speed. With the ball England's forwards won in my twelve games against them, I would have gone positively for attacking players behind.

It is easy to say all this when the job is not mine. As I say, I felt sorry for them that it never came right. It may be the turn of Wales to crumble in future. That is not as impossible as it might sound.

I have a debt to pay English rugby, to Roger White who taught me at Millfield; to players like Ricky Bartlett who came down to play against the school, to all the clubs who have entertained Cardiff so well and have given me a previleged time when I have been with them. After all is said and done, we are all one when it comes to the club-house.

I ought to tell how Englishmen helped me to get fit to play against their country at Twickenham in 1972. I was sure I would not be fit to play. The previous week I had suffered a kick in the back, and the bruising was deep.

It was my good friend Mike Summerbee, at the height of a dazzling football career with Manchester City, who invited me up to Maine Road. There everyone looked after me with great kindness. I had the benefit of modern physiotherapy equipment and all their professional knowledge of sporting injuries. I was soon declared fit and I was off to London, as good as new.

More importantly, I was suddenly in a confident

frame of mind. They had cosseted me in Manchester, made me feel important. I felt what every successful sportsman must feel, the confidence of knowing that I was a good player. It was not conceit. It was a thoroughly professional attitude which had rubbed off on me from Mike and his colleagues in one of the great fooball clubs.

12

Homeland

It is going to be impossible to write about Wales and the Welsh and mention everyone who has helped me or who has been kind to Maureen and me along the way. I could fill a whole book with names, end to end. I cannot do that. I hope I have said most of my thank yous face to face. No one must be offended if they cannot be fitted in here.

I have been lucky because my time in the Welsh international team coincided with a new era of coaching and talent. 1967, the year of my first cap, was the melting pot. Out of it came a coaching plan which made other countries apprehensive at first but then caught their approval. It was not easy. It did not happen overnight, but three years later, in 1969, we were beating Scotland 17–3, a luxury for Murrayfield, and taking the Triple Crown with home wins against the Irish 24–11 and against England 30–9. You notice how our scoring potential had increased and how success led to confidence and more success.

Winning at sport, especially at that level, is compulsory, second to none. In that period Wales were Grand Slam winners in 1971, 1976 and 1978; Triple Crown winners in 1969, 1971, 1976, 1977 and 1978. We won the Championship in 1970, 1971, a quintuple tie in 1973, and the Championship in 1975, 1976, 1977 and 1978. It reads well and now is the moment to relish it — when my feet are up on the mantelpiece.

Let me start with the coaching. Ray Williams was

appointed coaching organizer and, apart from going to work on the coaches themselves, he brought to the Welsh set-up a keener analysis of patterns of play and a reminder of the basics. In later years his assistant Malcolm Lewis also put a lot of effort and thought into the shop-window rugby played by the national team. Coaching did not transform my own game to any degree, but it certainly built into the Welsh players a deeper understanding of what we were trying to achieve, gave us confidence in our methods, made the smaller techniques more relevant and so gave us a capacity for absorbing pressure. It was almost as if panic stations were unnecessary because we knew what we had to be doing to play winning rugby. A mutually understood method was the crutch we leaned on. In many games our opponents took the lead first.

Selection theories changed too. A settled squad could organize itself as a fifteen-man unit on the international field, rather than fifteen units all hoping to be chosen for the next game. Out of this came a family feeling which showed itself in the pressure moments on the field.

Clive Rowlands was very intense as team coach, emotional and concerned. He was just the sort of motivator I needed in a dressing-room, thundering up and down, whipping up the patriotism. My blood was pounding by the time I got out there. Clive never said, 'We are going to play it like this today, or like that.' He saw that we had so many possible points of attack that he tried to reduce the game to simple concentration on the basics. He may not have been the greatest coach in the world, but he cared very much for the family and its motivation.

Coaching only emphasized what we should have known already. After all, unless you crossed the 'gain line', advantage line, or whatever they called it, in 1905 you never made any progress. Technically we digested more of other people's skills and tightened our own nuts and bolts.

I remember a lot of focus thrown on the points of possession. Winning the ball is better than waiting for it to be dropped by the opposition. I have never thought 'good' ball any different from 'bad' ball, though they became popular descriptions of possession gained. You have to be grateful for whatever ball you can get. I learned my lesson early at Millfield. I was playing for the school against a guest team which included some old internationls and county players. I was making a lot of noise, niggling away at my line-out jumpers when the ball was knocked back on the floor. Later, after the match when we were having a cup of tea, one of the opposition old hands had a word with me. 'Look here. It's all right for you cheeky little whippersnappers of scrum-halves to complain about the forwards, but let me tell you some of the problems your boys have.' He went on to explain how you could get an elbow in the eye, a knee in the groin, or even have sixteen stone standing on your foot, and that was without an opponent's hand going into the pocket of your shorts as you tried to leave the ground to make the catch.

From then on I have often called my forwards 'donks', but inwardly I have said, 'You get it anyhow, lads, and I'll try to do something with it.'

Of course throwing into the line-out was one of the major improvements of the new coaching because it lead to possession. It had always amazed me on the Lions South African tour of 1968 how Eric du Preez had outjumped the Scottish giant Peter Stagg. Now I could see what sheer coordination there had been between thrower and jumper. It was all in the timing between du Preez and Engelbrecht. Throwing is as important as jumping.

More than anything we understood that rugby was a simple game. Writers may like to imagine a web of improvisation and planning between Mervyn Davis and me at the base of the scrum, but it was simply an elimination of mistakes and accepting that we were as much a partnership as scrum-half and outside-half. Out of the harmony came the individual touches, but there was no long list of set moves.

My worry about Welsh rugby as I retire is that individuals will become too indoctrinated by coaching. Almost all the members of the Welsh teams with whom I played learned their rugby when there was no official coaching. We were all brought up to think of beating a man, selling dummies or side-stepping. Will there be another Gerald Davies now or will the young boy practise the crash-ball, taking a man out and the set moves of an automaton? That must never be, because stereotyped play can be countered too easily by positioning and tackling. The options are fewer when you cannot beat a man face to face. Coaches deny that they will stifle individuality, but I am not convinced. As I have mentioned, the success of the Welsh team from 1967 was as much to do with outstanding individual talents as with organization. Both were essential.

Although rugby is accepted as a running game, I admit I got a lot of pleasure from kicking. The kicking dispensation law made scrum-halves think hard about their tactical game, because they were always having to move quickly under pressure. Some started to run more but ended up sprinting backwards to the 25 in order to kick direct to touch. I was sad that the old touch-finding game had gone, because from my days with Bill Samuel I had always spent hours practising my screw-kicking both feet. Now we scrum-halves were faced with a simple choice, either we ran and got clobbered most of the time, or we gained ground by kicking on the bounce to touch. Obviously it was unwise to shovel every ball on to the outside-half.

Thus the grubber kick was given a whole new dimension. It became a kick for position. The screw kick would land on the point of the ball, the under-spun kick would often bounce backwards and the topped kick would roll on. The rolling ball was most effective as far as I could judge. It became an important strategy for the British Lions in South Africa in 1974.

The Lions in New Zealand in 1971 had superb backs but only a small share of possession. Therefore I needed to kick less if we were to play to our strength. In South Africa, our strength was our pack. If we moved the ball along the backs we were offering the Springboks a chance to see more of the ball than they would do in a straight forward battle up front. Also, if by passing we had not crossed the gain line or had been knocked over by the Springbok centres, just imagine the effect on the morale of the Lions pack. There can be nothing worse for forwards than to scrap for the ball, only to find, by the time you have picked your head out of the maul, that play has gone back fifty yards. So we decided to keep an iron grip on the South Africans, and the end justified the means. It won the series and that is why we were there.

I did not have to practise the grub kick very much because I had always been a touch player with my feet. Remember the soccer trial I had with Swansea Town. I enjoyed kicking too. I got really upset when I kicked the ball on the full touch.

Long kicks from scrum-halves are the quickest and most decisive way to turn defence into attack. That proved the case on my last visit to Twickenham in 1978. The ground was muddy and the rain had greased the ball. How could we get up to the English end of the field to break the 6-all deadlock? I managed to kick from our 25 to theirs, a long screw that torpedoed into the turf and sprung sideways into touch. We kept them there and ten minutes later Phil Bennett was kicking the penalty from thirty yards to win. One or two of the English boys that night grabbed me by the throat, play-fully of course, and said, 'You little Welsh b——, your kick was the one that killed us.'

What can I say of the Welsh players who have helped me through my career? From the start I was lucky to play under the protective eye of that big, strong forward Brian Thomas. He could hold them off; give you the calm ball in the middle of the storm. Then Delme

Thomas, the man with power and timing in the line-out jump. He was a hard man whom everyone respected. I only once saw him show a fist in anger because he did not have to prove himself that way. His talent came through.

John Taylor – now there was a good footballer who was surprisingly only given full credit when his international days were over. He was fast to the loose ball and always setting up the next move and thinking about the move after that.

I was lucky to serve my apprenticeship with David Watkins and Dewi Bebb. They were most encouraging. Then came the three players with whom I have spent most time in partnership, Mervyn Davies at number eight, and Barry John and Phil Bennett.

I must write about a great player and a great friend Gerald Davies. Gerald like D. Ken Jones was one of the most brilliant schoolboy centres. Then as the midfield became cluttered up with tacklers and spoilers he found more scope on the wing. He had always been fast. He had been a sprinter in Carmarthen Grammer School and most important, he was equally fast in rugby boots too. Not everyone is.

As for our friendship it stems from two facts. Gerald and I are from the same part of the Welsh-speaking world, and secondly I found that I could never go to the pictures without him because he is the only one who understood the plots! I could let my mind wander to the next day's game and, when I asked him about the flim, he knew every detail.

Life changed for Gerald, as it did for all of us, when time came to leave home. He went to Loughborough, became a Welsh international rugby player, but the most noticeable change came when he went up to Cambridge. Then we found his middle name Reames to be quite useful for the first time. Gerald Reames Davies was much more university. Soon we hyphenated it: Gerald Reames-Davies. He loved it, because he always possessed a quiet but subtle sense of humour. His choice of words was very apt, which is just about what you would expect from a man who was reading English at Cambridge.

I have to emphasize our backgrounds which were so very similar. Barry John had similar roots. We all three set out to achieve something and made it. It has given us an affection for each other. Grand Slams were not the essence of our dreams. It is just that all three of us played it the way we wanted and behaved as well with, I hope, a touch of individuality. What's more I love Gerald because he is prepared to listen to what I have got to say, rubbish or not! He rarely has an off-day as a person and a friend. People and things concern him.

He was, and still is, a sensational player. His side-step will be remembered by everyone who has seen it and certainly by those who have tried to prevent it. I recall a match we played up at Ellesmere College. Les Spence, one of our favourite Cardiff committee-men, took a side up there every year. This time, because we had such a strong team, it was decided to split the sides. Gerald and I were in opposing teams. Half way through the first half he got loose on the wing and I cut back to intercept him. I steadied myself in time to meet him face to face. I anticipated the famous side-step off the right foot. I lurked just inside to wait for it and also to drive him out towards touch. I was confident of stopping him. I got my geometry exactly right. In he came, but a split second later I was grasping thin air. It was not the angle that beat me, but the sheer speed. He could change direction by almost ninety degrees I knew that, but at ninety miles an hour! No one told me that.

As I say, Gerald's humour is quiet but well timed. We played England at Cardiff in 1977. Before the game the press had spent a lot of space writing about the record number of tries for an individual Welsh player. Gerald and I were tying, joint first on eighteen. It was a hard match but I managed to get over for a try in the second half. Gerald failed to score. It was a familiar set-up for me, a scrum five yards out from the English line on the right. Wales heeled the ball and I could hear the crowd baying in anticipation as it came to me. I had scored so many from that position, it had become almost automatic. I charged the line and over I went with a couple of defenders hanging on to me. It had worked again.

In the dressing-room later, one of the committee-men burst in and offered me his congratualtions for taking the lead in the try-scoring contest. Gerald, pale as ever, turned to me and protested with a straight face, 'Aw, c'mon Gareth, from a scrum-five, you're not going to count that one, are you?'

Gerald has been an exceptional captain of Cardiff. At first he was treated to lots of criticism, that he was too far away from the action on the wing and that Cardiff's play was not tight enough to be successful.

There will always be complaints like that, but I would like to point out exactly what Gerald Davies has done for the Club. Cardiff was once recognized as the greatest rugby club in the world. It was seen that way not only because of the results on the field, but for a whole range of qualities which mounted to the simple word – style.

I felt that from about 1970 onwards Cardiff began to lose that style bit by bit. No one was deliberately doing it, but nothing was being done to stop it either. For example, the hotel and travel economies had altered the character of the club. Trips to London had always included a night at a hotel and a good meal after the game. Other club sides could be seen charging up and down the motorways doing their best to save money for their clubs. I accept that Cardiff had to cut their cloth too, but the essence of playing for Cardiff was always that you played well in a talented side, felt good and behaved with style – which is different from living expensively.

On the field too I felt strongly that we had got away from the traditional style of playing. We had become less attractive and not all that more successful because of it. I am sure many committee-men thought I was just having a moan from time to time, but the reasons why I had wanted more than anything to join Cardiff as a young boy were disappearing. I was happy to make the noises but I was not getting anywhere with my opinions. Gerald Davies stuck to adventurous playing ideas even though he was severely criticized when Cardiff lost. He has set high personal standards off the field and spoken up in committee, and slowly we are recovering some of the intangible aura of being Cardiff members.

Why was I never captain of Cardiff? I was asked to stand once or twice, and again, in this year of retirement 1978. No, I never felt that I could take on the important commitments off the field, because I lived away at Porthcawl and worked further west in Neath. The one exception was the Centenary Year. My name was put up for approval by the players who chose by voting. On that occasion, 1975, I had taken the trouble to clear the year of all business ties, and once again Jack Hamer my patient employer said that he would back me up from the work point of view. I was the only name in the hat at first, but then Gerald was put up. He did not want to stand against me, but was persuaded, and I immediately remembered how Barry John had warned me against competing for the captaincy.

I was extremely disappointed on the night of the election not to win the vote. More than that, I was shattered. I had set myself up, shaped my views and given a lot of thought to training nights. That proves how seriously I had taken it, because training is not my strongest suit!

I remember getting into my car that night, wanting to drive away and not go back to Cardiff again in my life, not because I had lost an election for the captaincy, but because I had to assume that I was not popular with the players. That is always hard to take. Also I was angry that I had been put in that position in the first place, especially as I was competing against Gerald. Then, as I drove along the road into mid-

Glamorgan I suddenly felt a wave of relief sweep over me. By the time I got to my front door in Porthcawl I was able to say to Maureen, 'Gerald is the centenary captain, and that was a good choice.' I consoled myself with thoughts that it would have been almost impossible for me to do what I had set out to do.

Gerald's principles were firm and have not changed. We won no pots to put on the shelf, but the leadership and the support of equally strong men on the committee have put Cardiff back very close to where they were in my estimation.

Barry John was from Cefneithen, a small mining village which falls into the rugby catchment area overlorded by Llanelli. He was a great rugby player from a talented rugby family. Barry told both Gerald and me that he was packing up the game nine months before he did.

He was too young at twenty-seven to retire. He was going to become a better player, not worse, that is unless he had inside him a bug which gnawed away, telling him that life would be sweeter without the game. He probably did. Anyway Barry was nothing if not his own man, on and off the field, but I missed him and was sad that he went when he did.

I feel too, that Barry himself will not be at peace until Gerald and I have both followed him into retirement from international rugby. He must have identified with us so often from the grandstand, and all the more so because I do not think he gave his talent full expression. He will argue with me that he did. But I believed there were many more levels of maturity for him before the natural end came.

Those were my thoughts which I kept to myself at the time. I never tried to persuade Barry to play on. I recognized that he relished the business life ahead of him as a bit of a game and, as in rugby, the art is to be in the right place at the right time. Yet the happy-go-lucky lad on the surface was never as flamboyant underneath.

I never forget the first time we called him 'The King'. I had stayed at his home in Radyr on the outskirts of Cardiff, because the next morning our bus was to leave very early for London where we were to play the Harlequins. When we got to Cardiff Arms Park Ian Robinson and the boys asked me what sort of a house Barry had, because Radyr was known to be the watering hole of the barristers, surgeons and the like. 'Duw, Robbo,' I said. 'He lives in a sort of palace. He had to let down the drawbridge for me to get in . . . and d'y'know, there he was inside dusting his crown.'

'King John,' exclaimed Robbo. And that is how Barry John stayed.

Barry John was a match-winner. He generated confidence in other people. He could shrug off the bad days and, as far as I was concerned, he lived up to that boast down at Carmarthen in the early days of, 'Just chuck it and I'll catch it'.

Barry was a great player because he had talent first and foremost, but what people may not realize is that he cared. He was a competitor. There were sometimes jokes about his tackling, but he was always around when it mattered. Who will forget him having a go at stopping Dauga in Stade Colombes? Dauga did not score, Barry smashed his nose and went off. Even I thought I'd seen the last of him then. I was surprised to see him run on again, but then when he scored a superb try under the posts, there was no one on the ground who ever accused Barry John of being a butterfly.

'The King' was good for the Welsh side. Clive Rowlands once turned to Jeff Young in a squad training at the Afan Lido, Port Talbot. Clive announced some exercise on the beach if the conditions were right. 'Jeff, go down to the beach and see if the tide is in.'

'Better send Barry,' Jeff came back, ''cos if it's in he can send it out again.'

If Barry missed a penalty kick at goal in the tightest international, he would always come back muttering something about someone moving the posts. When he missed in New Zealand on the Lions tour, his own team could not believe it either. His accuracy was phenomenal.

Dropped goals too. I remember him dropping four goals to beat his old club Llanelli at Cardiff. We came off the field laughing and joking at the way we had won when suddenly through the crowd came an angry old man, sixty if he was a day, who declared himself a Llanelli fan. 'Should be ashamed to be a rugby player if you have to win matches like that, with drop goals.' As he finished his speech he whacked Barry straight in the face. Talk about the prophet in his own land.

Amateur players are sometimes subjected to so much criticism it is surprising how they survive. Phil Bennett, who took over from Barry, had been an exceptional player in the hard school of Welsh rugby, he had even played for Wales as a wing and a centre before he became the outside-half elect. How could he assume the kingly image? Nobody gave him a chance.

All I could see was that he had a big heart. He never let the comparisons and criticisms influence his game. Like Barry, but in a less flamboyant way, he did his own thing. He had a long fight to establish himself and I do not believe that he felt fulfilled in his own right until the Lions tour to South Africa. I remember him confessing then, 'You know, Gar, I'm only glad that we've done it, you and me. Nobody gave me a chance, and they were all telling you to retire when Barry went. But we've done it.'

The word great is thrown about. I have not done that. To me 'great' means the very top, the very best you have seen, and I would put Phil Bennett in that class.

Maybe he lacked self-confidence initially, and who would not? However, soon his experience as Llanelli captain began to show through. Phil has a quiet authority but firm nevertheless. His cover-tackling was eventually as much a feature as his running, which could be brilliant on his day. The pundits criticized his way of not running at his opponents and drawing them to him. I believe he was right to stick to his own style. With his ability with the ball in his hands anything can happen. He can turn a game on its end, and when he is not dodging away, splitting open the field, he is popping over a conversion from the touchline. There are winners and losers. Phil Bennett was a winner.

When Barry went, I thought my right arm had gone. Perhaps the selectors were going to play the club pair Clive Shell and John Bevan. I knew that what happened next could not be an overnight affair. To be successful I had to start another long relationship as I had done with Mervyn Davies and Barry John.

Phil Bennett came through it all as a man of guts and talent who led Wales to two Triple Crowns and a Grand Slam. I could throw the ball anywhere and he would not only pick it up but even turn a rolling ball to our advantage. He only kicked with his right foot – but who needs two feet when you have one as devastating as Phil Bennett's? It has all gone so quickly. It is hard for me to believe that I played with Phil Bennett as long as I did with Barry John. My partnership with Phil started as a left-over life, but it flourished and proved that when one king is dead, there are one or even two around the corner.

I say that because I was always happy to play with John Bevan. He was an easy partner, straight and direct in his approach, accomplished in every way. I had a lot of confidence in him and I hope he too felt that I gave him all the chances he wanted. I take my hat off to all my Welsh outside-halves, though there were only four. I had a deeper involvement with them than with other members of the team, rather like two troopers going to war. I shall never forget them and will always lift a pint to David Watkins, Barry John, Phil Bennett and John Bevan – not too short of talent that lot!

I once sat on the Welsh team selection committee, the

first captain to do so before or since. I was impressed by
the thoroughness. There was no emotion involved at all.
Everyone was calmly concerned with getting out the
best possible side for the nation.

There were many rumours at the time that if you
played for London Welsh you would get a cap. Harry
Bowcott was supposed to be the Svengali of the selectors fixing everything to put Old Deer Park on the map.
It is true that one or two did come in with the tide, but
London Welsh were a very successful club. They were
giving many of the top Welsh based clubs a run-around.
Their style of play was distinctive, and it was reasonable that their best players should be included in any
Welsh team which had ideas of playing fifteen-man-
attacking rugby.

As for Harry Bowcott, I always respected him and
enjoyed his company. Touring proved the finest opportunity for understanding each other. The outward
impression is that he is rather aloof and very much the
old Cambridge Blue, but both he and his wife were a
delight to be with abroad. His knowledge was sound
and his humour warm.

The other selectors on that unique occasion were
Rees Stephens, contributing so much to the discussion
of forwards, Jack Young and Vernon Parfitt offering
their experience as referees, Cliff Jones and Clive Rowlands on the subject of backs, and I believe I made
enough points on behalf of the players to earn my fine
dinner in the Angel Hotel, Cardiff. I was not asked to
join the selection meetings again, but then it became
less necessary as the coach became involved. The coach
could represent the players' ideas without worry of
involvement with friends among the players.

Nowadays the system has developed further to the
extent of Ray Williams and Malcolm Lewis, the full-
time coaching organizers, making their contributions.
They are not directly responsible but they do play a
large part in it, putting a lot of heart and effort into the
work with squads. I am sure I have driven poor Mal-

colm Lewis mad at training sessions. Sometimes I had enough after fifteen minutes and walked off. Malcolm would walk away in a huff. I treated Sunday training as if it was not my job – which is was not. Malcolm rightly put in the concern of a professional. I suppose we went our different ways asking sensible questions of ourselves; am I being fair to a man who had given up his Sunday, professional or not? Similarly Malcolm might have asked, 'Am I taking this all too seriously?' Whatever happened, it worked.

I keep coming back to this family feeling which grew with squad life. The family was not exclusive; there were often changes and new faces would be made to feel part of the set-up. It had the effect of reducing the amount of talk behind people's backs. If players had a moan they were invited to complain to an official. The 'them' and 'us' feeling, selectors against players, was gradually broken down. Bill Clement, the secretary, welcomed the new spirit. I even got a couple of bottles of champagne out of Bill towards the end. That, in rugby union terms, almost completed a revolution!

The captaincy of the Welsh team never stayed with me, as I have mentioned. Whenever there was an uncertain period of team-building to be done, I got the job then. There was a moment, however, when I might have inherited a new era. That was in 1975. I believe Clive Rowlands wanted me to take over, while John Dawes wanted Mervyn Davies. It was not an argument serious enough to split the camp, it was just that John knew Mervyn better, and Clive knew me. When John took over from Clive as coach he knew what he wanted. It was a tough job but he soon won credit. He set himself targets, and I remember him saying that if we came good by the last match of the 1975 season then he would be content. We did. Ireland were beaten 32–4 in Cardiff, and Mervyn Davies proved himself too as someone who could lead Wales by the example of his own play.

John Dawes always advocated that rugby football is a

game for the players. He was very protective of his men, as many press men discovered.

He always tried to play a fluid game, keeping the game simple and allowing players all the scope they wanted. I never had orders. He could impose tough training sessions on a squad but he was not a shouter. He had a quiet way of sorting out problems and, above all, had the vast experience himself both of playing and administration.

I never quite understood how his reputation sank with players and observers during the British Lions tour to New Zealand in 1977. Maybe both sides learned a bit.

I have loved the prestige that playing for Wales has brought me but the closest friends and the happiest memories have been with Cardiff; so many laughs, so many amusing people in the club. Cardiff stands for all that is good in the game. I explained how I believe that sights had been lowered for a while, but that happens to all clubs. As I leave the game I know I will not dream of leaving the Club, and hope to support and help where I can to keep the flag high. Such is its world-wide reputation we could accept a score of invitations to tour every year. How many clubs could have gone to South Africa and taken on Northern Transvaal and Eastern Province? How many could have gone to Rhodesia and have beaten a full Rhodesian side?

I am sad to see that there are problems in Rhodesia. That was the most enjoyable of all Cardiff trips. I would come out of retirement to go back there. As a touring party we owed a lot to our manager Colin Howe and committee-man Hadyn Wilkins.

This was in 1972, and we saw a life we never knew existed. A couple of moments are worth recording. Troutbeck was the most beautiful place I ever saw, a sort of Eldorado. The leaves of trees and bushes were richly green, the flowers breathtaking; paradise colours and smells. High above us was the faint blue outline of the Inianga mountains, its deep recesses changing colour with the occasional gliding cloud. I was in my heaven beside a lovely lake casting my fishing line across the surface. Was I dreaming? It was so calm and flat.

Then there came odd noises across the lake. I did not bother to look up. I guessed that a family of small animals or birds were quenching their thirst somewhere. No, it was laughter; hyena I thought. I looked up but the only intruder on the horizon was a rowing boat without oars or oarsmen. It floated closer and closer, and the laughing got louder and very boyish. Everything was still except for this laughing boat. It floated gently past me and I could not believe my eyes. There, side by side, on the bottom of the boat were two young Cardiff players. They were puffing on flimsy cigarettes and just laughing; the happiest men alive. They sounded almost delirious, and later it turned out that they probably were, because the locals had introduced them to pot. They looked so happy and smiling. They must have thought they had actually reached their heaven, and the chuckles drifted on and died away.

I can remember Ian Robinson being held firm over a crocodile pit about ten feet deep by Phil Kallonas. It was on a local crocodile farm and I must say I agreed with Robbo, the crocs looked ancient and half asleep. Robbo dangled his belt onto the crocodile's snout, clonking him with the buckle, but not a flicker, the old fella was half dead and uninterested.

They were just about fed up with that sport when suddenly the crocodile whipped up his head, jaws wide apart and cracked them together with a loud hollow snap. He just missed the hardy Robbo who leapt out of his skin. Cardiff nearly had to send for a replacement that day.

Memories of John O'Shea, a born comedian; of O'Shea and Howard Norris performing the Goon Show in the Wanderers Club, Johnnesburg. It will never be forgotten by those who were there. The members had never seen anything quite like it. Ageing colonels, card-playing ladies, everyone ended up rolling in the aisles.

The spirit of Cardiff's committee and helpers is typified by one delightful man, Les Spence. He must stand for them all in this book. Les was asked to manage the Welsh team on its tour of Japan. What a challenge for a man who had been imprisoned by the Japanese for a long period of war-time. How well he came out of it. He pushed his nightmares behind him and made the tour a joy for all of us. We used to tease him because his qualities of being accident-prone, a little clumsy and forgetful were loved by everyone. We used to say that he was the only manager who needed twenty-five players to look after him!

Speaking at one official reception he astounded even us by declaring, 'Gentlemen, this is my coach, Jack Daw,' pointing at John Dawes. Jackdaw has stuck with John, and Cardiff stuck to Les.

Finally, memories of the Cardiff boys singing their way quietly up the Zambezi river at dusk. It was then for the first time, with a few beers under my belt and a few songs to sing, that I realized a great rugby club had got under my skin.

13

To go or not to go?

Deciding to call it a day was such a strange feeling. I had often thought about packing it in, but I always played when September came around.

There was the moment when Barry John retired, and a lot of advisors said that I would never be the same without him. What they forgot was that I was two years younger than Barry; I was still only twenty-five. Then, especially in 1976 after Wales had won the Triple Crown and Grand Slam, some of my friends told me to get out, at the top. I spent that whole summer of '76 in a state of pretending retirement, knowing all the time that, come September, I would be puffing and panting up and down the pitch with the rest of the lads at Cardiff.

Ideas of retirement grew after the 1977 season. Wales had taken a second successive Triple Crown and a third British Lions tour stood before me. What stopped me going was that I knew from experience of the '71 tour to New Zealand just how much commitment was needed to win out there; how much punishment had to be taken, and how long I had to spend away from home again. This was it, I thought . . . the end is coming.

The autumn came; I was rotund and rested. I accepted an invitation from the South African Rugby Union to play for a selected World XV in their celebration matches. It was fun again in the company of many great players, and the old appetite came back. The rugby we played was on packed grounds. The Springboks hammered us, but my pride got me fit and once I had tested the water I knew that September would see me up to my knees in a new season.

It was only then that I seriously put my fiftieth Welsh cap in my sights. It would be a record. It was first mentioned by John Dawes out in Tokyo. We sat over a drink one day and he said it would be a fine achievement if I could make it, particularly as my appearances for Wales had been consecutive and unbroken. That was nice of him.

There is no way that you can play a full rugby season just for the sake of one international match. I played weekly for Cardiff and turned out for the odd invitation side. All went well until, surprisingly after a Welsh trial, I began to suffer a strange attack of nerves.

I was the young Edwards of 1967, afraid to get injured, terrified of loss of form or failure. I began to look after myself before club games, warming up and stretching to prevent the hamstring nightmares coming back.

Anyway I made it to Twickenham for the England match and when the day came I was as fit as I had been for any game. It was the bus ride to Twickenham which set my thoughts going again to retirement. That is when I first started to think about writing this book. I just felt that I would never pass that way again. When I faced reality in the dressing-room I simply wanted two things — for Wales to win and for me to get out on to the grass in one piece to get the record and forget it.

Phil Bennett gave me the ball to carry out. For a brief moment I wished it was Cardiff, but Twickenham was the second-best place. Many supporters have told me since that it was a shame the band was playing the Welsh anthem as I led out the team, so they could not cheer and sing at the same time. I was not aware of that. I had made it, but more important I said to myself, 'Surely we cannot loose? Not today, boys, anyway.'

I prayed as Alistair Hignell floated his final penalty

chance towards the Welsh posts – we only led 9–6 –
'Please God, don't let him spoil my day.'

It was a hard game but, always dreaming of the glory
road, typically me, I once spotted the chance to score
what would be a sensational try. We had taken play to
within five yards of the England line. This was it; if I
could scoop up the ball I was going to do the Steve
Austin bit, a bionic burst through everybody. The ball
was on the floor; it had squeezed out of the side of a
maul. I focused on it and the message flashed from
mind to body – the scoop – with one arm and the
ploughing drive over the line. In I went, down went the
arm and scooped but there was nothing there. It had
gone because just as I was about to lay a hand on it at a
hundred miles an hour, dear old Charlie Faulkner bent
down and hauled it back into the pack. 'Sorry, Gar.
Didn't see you coming,' he admitted so simply. I loved
him. If it had not been Charlie I would have torn a few
hairs out.

Wales did win – just, so the fiftieth cap had gone
well. The final whistle sounded and, of course by
instinct, I raced around looking for the ball. I really
can't help it; a sort of hypnotism takes over. I do not
know I am doing it . . . sometimes!

I discovered the ball under three of four forwards, all
scrapping for it. I managed to get a couple of fingers on
a panel. Mike Rafter was hanging on for dear life but
Charlie Faulkner was on top and Bobbie Windsor in
there too. 'Aw. C'mon lads. Let me have it this time,' I
said pathetically.

'Yes,' Bobbie chipped in. 'C'mon let's give it to
Gareth.'

It was such a strange situation. Everyone else had
gone off and there were the four of us left scrapping for
the ball surrounded by thousands of spectators who had
rushed on to the field. As soon as Mike was given room
to breathe he said, 'Yes sure. Its yours, Gareth.' I will
not forget that either. Poor Mike had a harder time
fighting for that ball with Faulkner and Windsor than

he had in the whole match.

On the coach afterwards I sat with Maureen. I was glowing. What a day for me and for all the boys. Then Maureen asked if I had read the telegram from my boys, Owen and Rhys. I simply had not had time to start on the messages, but when I told her that she was furious. I remember thinking, 'Fancy you're getting a rocket straight after playing your guts out in front of 70 000 people.' 'Look, love,' I explained, getting a bag full of telegrams down from the rack, 'You try and find it and read it. If I had done that I would still be in the dressing-room after the boys had played and come back again.' We laughed, started opening them there and finished them off later in the night.

In the team room, the management of our Kensington Hotel gave me a specially made celebration cake and I presented Gerry Lewis, the Welsh physiotherapist, with a special present. I had a clock set in anthracite coal, and inscribed, 'To Gerry. Thanks for making so many of the fifty possible.'

On to the Hilton and a superb banquet. The Rugby Union made a great gesture. On their behalf I was presented with a beautiful Spode porcelain bowl. It was number fifty. Funny, no one had ever presented me with one of those every time we beat England in Colbren Square!

I thought of lots of things that night. I did not want it to end. Where was Bill Samuel? He said he would be up for this one. Where was my brother Gethin? He told me he would be there, out on the terraces somewhere. My mother and father were in the stand, and so were my sister and brother-in-law. At one stage of the evening I dashed around to the London Welsh Society dinner and received a presentation. At five o'clock in the morning we were still going. We had a meal with a constant friend Stan Thomas, Stan Pies as he is known; eventually we returned to the hotel to find Max Boyce chatting night into day in the foyer.

The trip came to its end the next morning. I had

loved it. The committee, delighted by the win, allowed our wives to travel home with us on the bus. We stopped at Swindon for lunch; it was over.

Well not quite. At the end of this superb season which was to bring a Triple, Triple Crown and the Grand Slam, we were entertained by the Prime Minister, Mr Callaghan at 10 Downing Street. The next morning I got home and on the mat was a letter from the Welsh Rugby Union. It was a bill for £3.50 – 'lunch for wife at Swindon'. Well you must not expect everything to go your way, must you?

Deep down now I knew I would retire after this 1978 season. I had not actually sat down and made the decision, but I played against Scotland at Cardiff and, as with England, knew I would never see them again on the field. I wanted to savour every moment and I wanted Wales to be brilliant. I always had this dream of us totally fulfilling our natural flair at someone's great expense in an international. Sixty points to nil would have done.

All I got was a warning light. I was disappointed with my own game, and as an attacking force we lost our way after a promising lead had been gained. It was a reminder that international success does not just happen; you have to work for it. We must hit a higher plane in Dublin, I thought.

It was this Irish experience which dragged the decision to pack up from the secrecy of my guts to the confession in my mouth. I only told myself, but I believed me this time. We led Ireland by 13 points, yet somehow in a violent storm of green jerseys we were suddenly facing defeat with the score 13–13. That was the moment. I had a horror that 1970 was going to happen all over again. What a cheek I had, to imagine brilliant Welsh wins when we could hardly survive. My body ached. I looked to the stand and saw anger on the Irish faces as they seethed at the obstruction of Mike Gibson by J.P.R. I could see the Welsh party's serious, drawn looks. The last desperate effort turned out to be the great moment I was searching for; to soak up the pressure, to manufacture the try, to take the Triple Crown at Lansdowne Road. That was it – 20–16. It meant more than a showpiece, but now I knew I was done. No more Ireland for me.

The Welsh players themselves never truly worried about winning the triple Triple Crown. Cliff Jones had been chattering about it for many months. I suppose the achievement will eventually sink in. However, late on that afternoon in smart new dressing-rooms in Dublin I took an age to get dressed, and even when I left there were forwards still exhausted sitting around in their kit. Nobody said much. Bobbie Windsor dragged quietly in a corner on one of his roll-your-own cigarettes. Later, the lads wanted to go out on the town. I went to bed early.

Only I was aware that I was going to Cardiff Arms Park for the last time in a Welsh jersey, and I so much wanted to leave good memories of my play. I wanted to say a big thank you; I wanted to win, I wanted to show the world that I was too good to be upset by the bright new star, Jerome Gallion. Again that fear of failing came through. Only one home international had been lost in my career at Cardiff. That was against France, surely it was not to be again? What a way to go!

We won, the record says. We snatched the Grand Slam from France. We never got far enough ahead to lay on that demonstration of brilliance which I felt lay under the surface. There was no explosion. The prizes of the year had been great but we had to work for them, we had to go in and dig them out with our bare hands.

Then, when I walked off Cardiff Arms Park, 18 March 1978, I knew it was all over, though I suppose I will not be certain until I see someone else out there in the number nine shirt.

Coming off the field that day, Jean-Pierre Rives, my great friend and foe, had shook my hand in the tunnel as we made our way to the dressing-rooms. 'Gareth, you old fox,' he smiled. 'Next year in Paris.'

I said, 'Yes, Jean-Pierre, yes,' but I could not mean it.

The crowd clamoured around with their beer cans and scarves. One shouted, 'Australia next, Gareth, then New Zealand, and try and get South Africa so we'll be champions of the world.' That summed it up. That was as good a reason for deciding to retire as any — the Welsh rugby fans who are never satisfied. Within hours, others were trying to talk me into staying on to play against New Zealand, but that made no sense either. New Zealand would be just one more challenge. That would not be fair on me, nor on Cardiff, nor on Wales. Another season, another match, what could it do? I have since sat down in the comfort of retirement happy that I was part of a country which had rugby blood in its veins, and for a short time I was part of its national side which stretched out for the top and reached a pinnacle. I am thankful for that.

If you would like a complete list of Arrow books please send a postcard to P.O. Box 29, Douglas, Isle of Man, Great Britain.